Accounting for Life

Accounting for Life

HENRY BENSON, GBE, FCA

Lord Benson, of Drovers in the County of West Sussex

**KOGAN
PAGE**

In association with the Institute of Chartered Accountants in
England and Wales

At the request of the author, all royalties arising from the sale of this book will be made over to the Chartered Accountants' Benevolent Association.

First published in 1989 by Kogan Page Ltd, 120 Pentonville Rd, London N1 9JN in association with the Institute of Chartered Accountants in England and Wales, Chartered Accountants' Hall, Moorgate Place, London EC2P 2BJ.

Typeset by Litho Link Limited, Welshpool, Powys
Printed and bound in Great Britain by Biddles Ltd

British Library Cataloguing in Publication Data
Benson, Henry Alexander Benson. Baron, *1909-*
   Accounting for life.
   1. Great Britain. Accountancy — Biographies
   I. Title
   657'.0924

ISBN 0-7494-0029-3

Contents

List of Plates

Foreword

My motives for writing this account of some of the events of my life were simple. In the evening of my life I found I had the time, which had never previously been the case, and I wished to paint the picture of a chartered accountant in the hurly-burly of professional life in the twentieth century; to expose the demands which dedication to a profession involves; and to highlight some of the advantages and difficulties which can follow.

I do not know of any other book which tells, for those who are not engaged in the profession, how an accountant in practice in the United Kingdom carries out his work and the wide range of his activities. I think it was G K Chesterton who said there is nothing an Englishman enjoys so much as reading an account of something he already knows all about. For this reason I hope the ensuing pages may also have an interest for some members of my profession because they will recognise many aspects of professional life, which, in greater or lesser degree, have affected their own careers.

Except for a year or two of misery when, raw and unsophisticated, I first came to wet and foggy London from warm and sunny South Africa at the age of 17, my life has been happy and at times exciting. I have enjoyed it to the full. I have never been idle and I become restive and uncomfortable if I have nothing to do. Most of what I have had from life I owe to my parents, the education I had in my first years as a schoolboy, the discipline and training of a chartered accountant and, last but not least, my marriage. As soon as one reaches a certain level, the profession of accountancy provides for its members responsibility, interest, and a variation of work which is matched by few other occupations. I recommend any young person who has a normal intelligence to join it, provided that he or she is willing to work very hard and is able to become proficient in speaking and writing the English language.

The use of the English language is a theme which runs through the following pages. As in every profession, the task of an accountant is to diagnose the problem and then to explain it, and the proposed remedy, to the client. It is not merely a question of grammar and syntax, but the skill of expressing thoughts simply and clearly. It is the hallmark of a good professional and it commands the respect and confidence of the public.

The importance of this was exposed to me quite early in life. My firm was concerned with a complicated Trust Deed and application to the Court was necessary to find a solution. Five separate Counsel represented different, conflicting interests. The first four spoke to their briefs at great length, at the end of which the Judge was confused and irritable. Cyril Radcliffe KC (later Lord Radcliffe) then rose to his feet. He began in this way: 'I wonder if your Lordship would allow me to address you for a few minutes.' His silver tongue and polite opening reduced the temperature in the Court at once. Then, speaking slowly, in a few short, lucid sentences he explained the problems and urged the Court towards the solution he himself favoured. It sounded clear and obvious, but I have no doubt that Radcliffe had spent many hours, if not days, in preparation before he had felt ready to address the Court. From the time he first opened his mouth I felt that the issue was never in doubt and that Radcliffe would get his way. And so it proved when judgement was given.

If, in the twenty-first century, some budding accountant strays across this volume in the Institute library, I am sure he will say to himself, 'It was all quite different then. Things don't happen that way now'. As he matures in the profession I think he will find he is wrong. I have noticed that the basic professional principles which were laid down by the Cooper brothers in 1854 have remained unchanged all through my lifetime, and I do not think they will alter much in the years to come. It is only the outward trappings that change.

Henry Benson
London, 1989

Acknowledgements

I express my warmest thanks to partners, staff and other colleagues all over the world who, in one way or another in the sixty-three years since I began life as an accountant, have helped me in the events described in these pages. This book would not have been written without them.

The cartoons by David Myers are reproduced by the courtesy of *Punch*.

1.

The Family Influences

The reader who has been sheltered from the rough and tumble of finance and figures may like to know the characteristics of an accountant and the motives which inspire him. The best description I know (attributed to H L Mencken, an American man of letters) was sent to me many years ago by a client who felt aggrieved by some advice I gave him.

> The typical auditor or accountant is a man past middle age, spare, wrinkled, intelligent, cold, passive, non-committal, with eyes like a codfish, polite in contact, but at the same time unresponsive, cool, calm, and as damnably composed as a concrete post or plaster of paris cast; a human petrification with a heart of feldspar, and without charm or the friendly germ, minus passions and a sense of humour. Happily, though, they seldom reproduce – and all of them finally go to Hell.

The ensuing pages will show how well I fit this mould. In writing this account of myself I face the difficulty that the relations between a professional man and his client are confidential. Many of the events in my life which might be of interest to the public cannot therefore be told. I have written, for the most part, about public or semi-public work of one sort or another and in some places I have omitted names to avoid giving hurt.

I was born in Johannesburg, South Africa, where my parents lived. My father, Alexander Stanley Benson, was one of the sons of Alexander Benson, an Irishman who took a degree at Trinity College, Dublin at the late age of 27. He became a parson in the Church of England and for thirty-one years was vicar in the village of Loppington in Shropshire. My father left home after taking a degree at Cambridge and went to South Africa, where he became a teacher at St Andrew's College, a boy's school in Grahamstown. Just before the outbreak of the Boer War, he became the head of St John's College, Johannesburg, but it was a short-lived appointment. The official history of the school says that 'he took over for a time until one day the handful of boys arrived and found no master. Hearing that he was about to be arrested Benson had left the previous night (by bicycle) to join the British forces.' In those days the judges in South Africa were appointed from London and one of them who went out shortly after the Boer War was Leonard Syer Bristowe. After the Boer War my father beame clerk to Leonard Bristowe in Pretoria.

My mother was Florence Mary Cooper, one of the daughters of Francis Cooper. I shall recount later some of the history of the firm of Cooper Brothers & Co, a London firm of chartered accountants, and Francis was one of the four brothers who between them were responsible for building up the firm which began in 1854. Francis Cooper was one of a family of thirteen. His father was Emmanuel Cooper, a staunch Quaker and a vigorous anti-slaver who worked to that end with William Wilberforce. I still have a few pieces of 'slave' china which were made at that time and were adorned with pitiable pictures of slaves in order to remind the public of their plight. Francis complained that he and his brother, Ernest, who were the last of the thirteen, never got enough to eat and he ascribed his subsequent afflication of diabetes to a shortage of food in his early years. He died aged 48 in 1893.

There is a sad tale attached to Emmanuel Cooper. He was one of the founders in 1836 and, for the early years, chairman, of the London and County Bank, which later became part of the National Westminster Bank plc. The firm of Cooper Brothers & Co and my family, have always banked with the National Westminster, or its predecessors under different names, and I was asked one day to lunch with the directors in Lothbury. In the course of conversation, and with some pride, I mentioned Emmanuel Cooper and his early association with the bank. The secretary of the bank was kind enough to say that he would look up the records. He telephoned a day or two later and asked in a rather round-about way whether I really wanted to be given all the details. I said, 'What's wrong? Did he pinch the cash?' There was a long pause at the other end, after which I was given to understand that there were some 'unfortunate details'. I asked for these to be sent to me, from which it emerged that Emmanuel advanced himself some money and could not, and did not, repay it. The amount was about £16,000 which was a substantial figure in those days. He was dismissed from office and died in 1851 aged 57. The records conclude with a pitiful letter from his wife asking for some money to keep her from penury, but the request was bluntly turned down. The complaint by Francis and Ernest that they did not have enough to eat in their childhood days may well have been justified. Whatever Emmanuel's faults may have been, he left an injunction to his family to 'hold together as a bundle of sticks which cannot be broken' and I think that, in my end of the family, we have done so.

My grandmother, Francis Cooper's wife, and Mrs Leonard Bristowe were sisters and had the maiden name of Power, and in 1905 my mother went on a holiday visit to South Africa to stay with her aunt in Pretoria. My mother met my father on this visit and in due course they were married in the cathedral in Pretoria in 1906. My sister, Pamela Brenda Benson, was born in 1907 and I was born on 2 August 1909 and was given the names Henry Alexander. About the time of his marriage my father set up in practice as a solicitor in Johannesburg and, apart from a short and unsuccessful foray into farming, continued in practice until his death.

As a family we were not well off but were never in serious want or hardship. I went to school at an early age at St John's College preparatory school in Johannesburg. The college was mainly staffed at that time by the Mirfield Fathers. Their influence declined in later years but the school has always

prospered and it was then, as it is now, one of the great
private schools in South Africa with a strong religious
background based on a profound belief in the Christian
faith. The teaching in the preparatory school was first rate;
for two or three years I was taught by a Miss Thomas and
any success I have had in life is largely due to her. She was a
stern disciplinarian and accepted nothing but the best. She
taught me to concentrate and drummed into me the need
always to attain the highest possible standard; in these
respects my parents were her enthusiastic supporters. I did
well in the preparatory school but tailed off when I went up
to the college. My parents (influenced in part I think by a
shortage of cash for school fees) therefore took me away and
sent me to Parktown High School. Most of the schooling in
South Africa was at that time, and is now, undertaken by the
government and was provided free except for some trifling
contributions from the parents. Parktown High was a new
government school when I joined it in 1921 and there were
some rough characters in the early intake. It was despised by
the other established schools but gradually, under the
leadership of a strong headmaster, P M Druce, it took shape
and in a few years was as good as any of the others and this
is still so today. The teaching at Parktown was good. I have
been all over the world and have moved in all levels of
society but I have never felt myself at a disadvantage for lack
of a good early education. Whenever I go to South Africa I
visit both St John's and Parktown High and have from time
to time addressed the school at both places. I have told them
the gratitude I feel for the teaching which I was given in both
places and how much of my life has been influenced by it.

We had a happy home life but shortage of money
sometimes caused minor upsets. My mother was a strong
character for whom I had the greatest respect and affection
and she, like Miss Thomas, influenced my early life. I
attribute the good health I have always enjoyed, and the
energy which flows from it, to her insistence that up to quite
a late age I should go to bed at 6 pm. Young children
nowadays stay up until 7, 8, 9 o'clock, and even later,

watching the 'telly' and I believe this impairs their health, now and for the future. My father was a warm but at times irascible character. He had a first-class brain and was a strong courtroom lawyer but I doubt whether he administered the financial aspects of his practice to the best advantage. He had a passionate belief in the proper use and elocution of the English language and I shall always be grateful for his insistence that I should follow his example; it has stood me in good stead in my professional life. In 1920 he decided to cease practice and to go farming. He bought an orange farm between Pretoria and Rustenburg, about fifty miles from Johannesburg. In the first year or so we lived in tents in a good deal of discomfort while the house was being built. My father carried out a lot of the woodwork himself and I helped him in the holidays; this taught me the elements of carpentry which became a relaxation for me in later years. He was an ardent beekeeper. The African bee is more aggressive than her English cousin and, despite veils and gloves, the family always suffered from bee stings when one of us was required to help him inspect the hives or take off the honey. In a good year we would extract from the combs three-quarters of a ton of honey – much of it gathered from the blossom of thousands of orange trees in the vicinity. We eked out a precarious living on the farm for four or five years but it was not a success and my father returned to practice in Johannesburg in 1925 and continued as a solicitor until his death in 1931. After we returned to Johannesburg, my parents used to lend the house on the farm to relatives for holiday purposes. The roof was of thatch and during one such period the African servant piled a heap of dry timber on the kitchen grate. A spark shot up into the roof which caught fire and the house was completely destroyed, except for the outside walls, in about twenty minutes. This was a grievous blow because the house was not insured and there seemed little prospect of ever being able to restore it.

My sister, Pamela, began to teach as soon as her formal education was finished and she remained a teacher in government schools all her life. She never married, but in 1947, when my wife and I were in Johannesburg on the business of New Union Goldfields, my wife persuaded her to adopt a child in order, among other things, to relieve in due course the loneliness of old age. It would never now be permitted for a single woman to adopt a boy of three, but it was allowed then. It might have been a failure, especially as my sister was teaching all day but she lived with my mother who helped in the upbringing. The adoption turned out to be a great success. Brendan Alexander Benson went to St John's College in Johannesburg and then to an agricultural college in Natal. In those years the farm yielded no income, but by pinching and scraping, my mother and sister somehow managed to keep possession of it and in due course rebuilt the house on spartan lines. When Brendan finished at agricultrual college he took over the management of the farm, which has prospered under his care. In 1981 he married and he and his wife Emma are now raising a family in the house which he has rebuilt with modern equipment and conveniences. It is sited on the foothills of the Magaliesburg mountains with a view, on a clear day, stretching many tens of miles to the north. It is a nostalgic experience for me when I go back there now. Since leaving South Africa in 1926 I have never wanted to return to live there permanently, but I realise what an enormous affection I have for the land of my birth and the emotional hold that it still has over me.

I have watched the political scene in South Africa with growing distaste and alarm. When I was a child the social division between the blacks and the whites was complete. The Africans were a subservient class and were not permitted by law to carry out certain types of skilled work; they were not allowed into hotels or public buildings except as servants; on the trams they were permitted to sit only in a special area on the upper deck in the open; and, in the trains, separate coaches were provided for them. Every black had to be given a written 'pass' by his employer to enable him to be out after dark. If black and white met on the pavement the black moved on to the road. It would have been unthinkable at that time for an African to be a pupil at any of the government or private schools. Much has changed, of course, and many of these restrictions have been removed, with the result that blacks and whites move about freely in the shops, hotels, places of business and entertainment and the pass laws have been abolished. Nevertheless, the bulk of the white Afrikaner population still cannot regard the African as anything but a subservient race. Apartheid cannot be justified on moral or common-sense grounds and, in my view, is bound to fail in the long term because with a population of some 5 million whites and over 20 million blacks, each dependent on the other, it is ridiculous to believe that segregation can be a permanent way of life. The risk is that the end will come not by political change but by bloodshed.

I do not think that the public at large who have never visited South Africa realise the problems which beset it. South Africa contains within its borders two separate civilisations – a First World comprising the white and the Third World comprising the black. One has only to look at the Third World countries in the rest of the globe to realise how long it will be before any Third World country can bring itself up to First World living conditions; this seems to be what the ill-informed outside world want and expect to happen almost overnight. The changes which have to be introduced in outlook, customs and habits, the abolition of witch doctors, pagan attitudes, language, plural marriages, administration and systems of government, are enormous. Tribal customs and rivalry run very deep in the African mind and often lead to bloodshed. We have only to remember the tribal attitudes which prevail among the English, the Welsh and the Scots, and the fierce nationalistic outlook of some of them, to appreciate the deeper problems which face a backward African population.

I have watched ,what has taken place over a period of eighty years and have seen how slow the progress can be. The problems of education and housing alone will create enormous burdens on the economy. Even if the process of change started tomorrow, with enthusiasm and the best intentions, I think it would take two or three centuries rather than years before South Africa could become a multi-racial society with equal opportunities for the whole population, irrespective of colour or creed.

Kenya has enjoyed independence since 1963 and is administered under a government dedicated to the advancement of the African population. One only has to move into the primitive conditions in the country districts, however, to realise how little the situation has changed in twenty-six years and how many scores of years it will be before divisive tribal customs are eradicated and education and housing reach an acceptable level if judged by modern standards. I think the Masai child will still be walking barefoot, clothed with a blanket and armed with a spear in the year 2100. The position in the neighbouring territories which have been given independence – Tanzania, Uganda, Zimbabwe, Zambia and Malawi – is little different and in some cases worse.

At the end of 1923 when I was 14, my mother's sister who lived in England became very ill. My mother wished to see her before she died so she took a quick and cheap trip home on the SS *Ceramic*, a ship which had an honourable record in the Second World War before she was sunk by the Germans. I was allowed to accompany my mother and this visit settled my future life.

In London on the last day of the visit my mother and I had nothing to do and she suddenly said, 'Let's go down to the office.' The office meant the office of Cooper Brothers & Co in the City. Before she left for South Africa my mother had been brought up with most of the then partners and she thought she would like to see them again. We arrived without notice and a difficult half-hour followed. The partners remembered my mother very well but they had not met for fifteen or twenty years so it was hard to find common ground for conversation. In desperation, Stuart Cooper, my mother's cousin, said, "Well, Florence, if you want this lad to come here when he has finished school we will take him.' We left soon afterwards and, as we crossed the threshold, my mother said, 'That settles it then. As soon as you finish school, you will come here.' This decision was never questioned by me or anyone else. I left school in December 1925 at the age of 16 and worked for a few months as an office boy in my father's office at £4 a month. One of my few responsibilities was to keep the postage book, but it never balanced, and at the end of the week there was always an entry 'sundries' to make up the difference. In October 1926, a couple of months after my seventeenth birthday, I found myself in London under articles (as they were then called) to become a chartered accountant.

Life under articles then was very different from the present studentship of budding chartered accountants. Most of my contemporaries, like myself, joined straight from school and it was rare for an articled clerk to have a university degree. Parents who wanted their sons to be articled had to pay a premium to the firm and at that time Coopers' charged 500 guineas. It was remitted in my case because of my family connection and in any case I think we would have had difficulty in finding the money. Articled clerks were not paid a salary but something under one half of the premium was normally returned over the period of articles of five years. I received a cheque for £10 at the end of the first year, which I sent home as a set off to the allowance my parents were paying me. The payment at the end of the following year was increased to £15. In the last three years of articles I received a total of about £250. On qualification in 1932 I was put on the firm's payroll at £250 a year, which was £25 more than was paid to other newly qualified chartered accountants who had joined the firm. I assume the family connection was responsible for the difference.

We worked in the office all day and on Saturday mornings. The studies for our examinations were provided by a system of correspondence courses with one or other of the private teaching establishments formed for that purpose and we paid the fees out of our own pockets. In order to pass the examinations, several hours of work per day had to be carried out in one's own time at home. I set myself a rough standard of ten hours a week, later increased to fifteen when the examinations drew near. The training establishment I joined was E Miles Taylor, which was well known and popular with articled clerks; it used to repay the course fees to anybody who got 'honours' in the Institute's examinations. I achieved this in the final examination and on the day I passed, I called on Miles Taylor to collect the cheque as I needed the money to help me to get back to South Africa to my visit my family. He wrote out a cheque there and then and added a welcome bonus of £10.

Times have changed. It is now rare to recruit students who do not have a good university degree and entry direct from school, though not impossible, is the exception. There is competition among the big firms of accountants to secure high-quality students so that anyone who has had a good school and university record can more or less pick whichever firm he or she thinks will provide the best training and prospects. In my day Coopers would never have dreamt of giving articles to a woman and the number of women in the whole student body of the Institute was minimal. Nowadays between 30 per cent and 40 per cent of the people who are accepted as students are women and the figure is continually rising. Students are paid a salary on joining which at the time of writing is between £9,000 and £10,000, although at that stage they are little more than a pair of hands because their knowledge of practical auditing and accountancy is minimal. Correspondence courses are a thing of the past and the teaching of students is undertaken in-house by the firms that take them as students. This places an enormous burden of overheads on practising firms of accountants. The annual cost in any of the big eight firms of accountants in the UK runs deep into seven figures.

My early years in London were a misery. I lived alone and rent free on the top floor of a house which my grandmother (Francis Cooper's widow) owned but did not occupy in Westbourne Gardens near Royal Oak station. My allowance from home was £10 a month, so there was nothing to spare for amusement or entertainment and in consequence I did not go out at night or have any social contact in the evenings. The change from sunny South Africa to foggy London with short winter days was acutely depressing. With a bit of a struggle I could manage to get by on the money which was available, but I was desperately lonely on my own in London and in a highly nervous state. My grandmother lived in Reigate and fortunately I was able to stay with her at weekends, otherwise I would have been in poor shape. I do not regret this period of my life although it was the unhappiest which I have ever spent. It did me no harm in the long run and among other things it has made me sensitive to the loneliness which is suffered by many people, young and old. Later on things improved greatly; my allowance from home stopped, but my mother's brother, Francis D'Arcy Cooper, son of Francis Cooper, took me under his wing and gave me an allowance of £250 a year until I qualified.

One of the advantages of being on short commons during my articles was that I had few distractions in the evenings and applied myself to my accountancy studies. I passed eleventh in the intermediate examination and fourth place in the final out of 1,088 candidates. The first place was taken by Stanley Duncan, who later became senior partner of Price Waterhouse, and the fifth place was taken by R G Leach (later Sir Ronald Leach GBE) who became senior partner of Peat Marwick Mitchell and President of the Institute of Chartered Accountants. The three of us saw a good deal of each other in later years. I qualified as a chartered accountant in 1932 and on 1 October 1934, at the age of 25, I was made a salaried partner in Cooper Brothers & Co at £1,000 a year. This early admission to partnership would not have happened but for the family connection and it was a clear case of nepotism, but at that time all the partners except one were getting on in years and they needed some younger blood. I happened to be in the right place at the right time.

D'Arcy Cooper was a remarkable man and is another of the people who influenced my life enormously. He and his wife had no children. He became a partner in Cooper Brothers & Co in 1910 and joined up at the outbreak of the First World War in the Royal Artillery. He was badly wounded but survived after some anxious days. In 1919 he returned to the firm and began to reorganise the whole of its practice. He took over the work of Lever Brothers Ltd which had been a client of the firm since 1887. In that year William Hesketh Lever (later Viscount Leverhulme) went to see his bankers in London, the District Bank Ltd, later absorbed by National Westminster Bank plc. He sought the advice of the general manager, Tom Henderson, because he felt that the size of his business in the north of England had grown to such an extent that he needed the services of a London accountant. Henderson took him round to see my great uncle, Ernest Cooper, with the result that ever since that time the company and the firm have lived through triumph and disaster together; this has built a happy association, which now extends for a period of over one hundred years. It was said unkindly at that time by his professional colleagues that Ernest Cooper was greatly impressed by this introduction and was so anxious to secure a permanent source of good clients that he married Henderson's daughter. This was quite untrue, and it would have been an incestuous arrangement in any case, as Henderson was already his brother-in-law.

In 1921 D'Arcy Cooper was called in by Lever to solve the crisis facing the recently acquired Niger Company. Because of a worldwide fall in raw material prices, the overdraft and working capital problems facing the Niger Company were acute and its bankers were threatening to issue a writ. Liquidation seemed the inevitable consequence when D'Arcy Cooper arrived on the scene and, in the words of Charles Wilson, Unilever's official historian, 'holding off the creditors with one hand he negotiated with the other terms for a loan from Barclays Bank – terms which, though onerous, were yet to prove the salvation of the Lever Group'.

In 1923 Leverhulme asked D'Arcy to join the board of Lever Brothers. D'Arcy told me that he had wished not to go, so he proposed terms which he felt would be prohibitive. History has it that the afternoon the letter was received, Leverhulme telephoned with the single message 'Come at once'.

It was fortunate he did so. As an industrialist Leverhulme had been a great leader and expansionist and he was foremost in recognising the importance of industrial relations and the need to provide good conditions and opportunities for the work force at all levels. In the early 1920s, however, his genius was on the wane and the business was not in good shape. D'Arcy took a grip of the situation and, when Leverhulme died in 1925, became chairman. An indication of the low ebb which the company had reached is provided by the accounts published in 1926, which show that the total reserves from all sources amounted to £22,600 8s 6d. D'Arcy spent the early years in reorganising the structure and cutting out the dead wood and in 1929 brought about the merger with the Dutch firm Margarine Unie; thus Unilever Ltd and Unilever NV came into being.

D'Arcy was a natural leader of men. His commanding presence, business acumen, integrity, common sense and humour combined to make a man who inspired respect and affection. I admired him as much as any person I have ever met and count myself lucky to have been so close to him and to have benefited from watching his character and powers of leadership. He was made a baronet in 1941 and died later that year at the relatively early age of 59. In due course after the Second World War I took over the Unilever work which was undertaken by the firm. I have always had a special interest in its affairs and have been a close friend of the Leverhulme family and the grandchildren and great grandchildren of its founder. Unilever has just celebrated its centenary and it can look back over the past hundred years at a remarkable record of successful industrial enterprise. Apart from the difficult period after the First World War, it has shown continuous growth and prosperity worldwide. In

1987 the total turnover was £16,550 million and the total reserves (which compares with the figure of £22,600 quoted earlier) just short of £3,000 million.

After I was made a partner I became interested in my leisure time in the work of the Victoria League, which was concerned with providing help and contact for students from the colonies and dominions who came to London to study. In June 1939 I attended one of their periodical dances when I met Anne Virginia McLeod. She decided that I could not dance (a view which she has consistently and correctly held since that time), but we found common ground in other subjects and soon afterwards became engaged. By August 1939 it was evident that war would break out and everyone realised that life would be disrupted. Young able-bodied people expected to be drafted into the Services, which might involve long periods overseas. There was thought to be an imminent risk of bombing in London and other cities, though in fact this did not take place until later. The use of gas by the enemy was expected and in the early days we were all required to carry gas masks wherever we went. Jinny and I felt that, as our lives were bound to be subject to major upsets in one way or another, we might as well enjoy what we could in whatever time was left to us, so we got married on 2 September 1939, at St Mary Abbotts in Kensington, the day before war broke out.

Our elder son, Peter was born in November 1940 and twins, Michael and Phyllida, in May 1943. I was anxious for my sons to have the benefit and disciplines of a public school and originally had Rugby in mind. However, a brother officer in the Grenadiers, John Glyn, who had himself been to Eton, persuaded me that Eton was altogether better. In due course both boys went to Maidwell, a preparatory school in Northamptonshire and when they had passed their common entrance, to Eton.

When Peter left school he spent some months in Madrid learning Spanish and then took a degree at Edinburgh University. He was articled to the firm and became a chartered accountant; he is the fourth generation to be a partner and the only descendant of the original Cooper brothers now in the firm. After leaving Eton, Michael spent a tough year as a jackaroo in Australia. He then spent some years with Lazard Brothers & Co Ltd and later joined Standard Chartered Merchant Bank Ltd, a subsidiary of the Standard Chartered Bank. When Phyllida left school, she went to America for several months where she kept herself by finding work. She began in Boston but soon moved to the larger excitements of New York and later to Mexico. She married Simon Dare, a chartered accountant who was for some years with the Union Discount Company of London plc and later joined Clive Discount Co Ltd.

In about 1956, when my sons were at Eton, the school was going through a bad patch. Several parents had, independently, come to the conclusion that the teaching and curriculum needed improvement and that they had not been amended to meet post-war conditions. Most of the fathers had themselves been educated at Eton so they could speak with authority. We met together to discuss it. One mother had been particularly enraged when she complained to the housemaster that her son was not being taught English properly. The housemaster did not please her when he replied, not with humour, that 'English is only for baboons'. I went to see the headmaster, Robert Birley (later Sir Robert Birley) in his study at Eton. The desk was piled high with exercise books which he was marking; he showed some of them to me and explained how deeply he was concerned in the teaching. I was not impressed because I felt that a headmaster of a very large school should be less concerned with the minutiae of teaching and be spending the bulk of his time on administration and organisation. Robert Birley later met the parents in London but the meeting got nowhere. The matter then escalated to include the Provost and Fellows. I received a letter from C F Cobbold (later Lord Cobbold), the then Governor of the Bank of England who was a Fellow of the college, saying he felt that the complaints were not justified, but he invited the parents to a meeting at the Bank of England to discuss it further.

One of the mothers who came to the Bank was accustomed to deal with the manager of her local bank in Surrey and was not familiar with the hierarchy of the City. When the doorkeeper in his top hat and pink tail coat asked whom she wished to see she said, 'I have come to see the manager.' Much dialogue ensued before the doorkeeper realised that the person she was asking for was the hallowed and remote figure of the Governor himself. In fact the meeting was not taken by Kim Cobbold but by another Fellow of Eton, Sir Edward Bridges (later Lord Bridges). The complaints were noted and in due course changes were made. By that time, however, our sons had left, or were leaving, for other pastures, but perhaps less well equipped than they might have been.

Each of my children has two daughters and a son so that my wife and I have nine grandchildren. I have always had a profound belief in the strength and comfort of home life and the lasting advantage of staunch family ties. For that reason I have recently had pleasure from overhearing a remark made by one of my teenage grandchildren: 'I don't want anything when grandpa and grandma pop off except their photograph albums.' When my three children finished school in 1961, we thought that would be the last year when we would all have a family holiday together and that some extravagance was justified. I therefore chartered a sailing boat in Athens and we spent a fortnight cruising in the warm sunshine and blue seas of the Greek islands. By good fortune this was very far from being the last holiday we all spent together. As things have turned out our children and grandchildren have been with us on holiday on many occasions. In recent years my wife and I have taken a lodge on the edge of a loch near the Findhorn river in Scotland in August, and the whole family – children, grandchildren and their friends – gather there in a great heap. They sail, play golf and tennis, bathe in the sea, picnic, fish, make barbecues, walk, squabble and laugh together. The Zulu word for a meeting at which much talk takes place on tribal affairs is an *ndaba*. The decision as to whether we should go back to the same place each year does not rest with me. It is the subject of a family *ndaba* and happily so far the decision, *nem. con.*, has always been to do so. I am no fisherman and the Findhorn is a dour river in August. By a long chain of circumstances, which does not warrant repetition here, I have lashed the waters of the Findhorn, on and off, since 1936. It was not until 1988, fifty-two years later that I caught a salmon there – much to the astonishment of myself, my family, the locals and, I suspect, the fish. It must be the most expensive salmon that has ever been grassed in Britain; it was a modest achievement of seven and a half pounds.

In 1973 I took all the children and their spouses to East Africa on a tented safari which opened their minds in many ways. In 1987 the children felt that they would like their own children to enjoy the same experience and we decided on a special venture together. All of us, including a teenage friend, making a total complement of eighteen, went on safari and lived under canvas in Kenya to see the animals in their natural state. The age range of the party was from 78 to 6. Between us we took about 3,600 photographs of animals, birds and the local scenes. My elder son, Peter, made a photographic record in a form which can be played back on video. I hope that these will be looked at with pleasure, and sometimes hilarity, for two or three generations to come.

We saw a great quantity of game and bird life and were lucky to see two incidents which were out of the ordinary. In the Samburu Reserve we came across a cheetah basking in the sun. She was great with child and the accouchement was clearly due in a day or two. Cheetahs seem to enjoy being the centre of attention, and this one posed for us first in one way and then another, finally rolling over on to her back in complete abandon. Suddenly she whipped round and crouched down with every sinew taut. We were puzzled by this, until we saw a lioness walking nonchalantly down the hill. When she got to within fifty yards she saw the cheetah and froze. The two animals had a hostile eyeball to eyeball confrontation for about thirty seconds, at the end of which 'Ms Lioness' decided to attack.

Cameras clicked at a tremendous rate, but it is not easy to get a charging lioness into focus. It was an unequal contest. The cheetah is probably, for short distances, the fastest animal on four legs, and in 150 yards the expectant mother, despite her encumbered state, had outdistanced her pursuer.

Later that week we noticed an African eagle moving every now and then from treetop to treetop, but did not attach much importance to it. We then came across a gerenuk, which is a dainty brown antelope with a long neck, rather like a miniature giraffe without the spots. It has no defence against predators except speed and camouflage. The gerenuk had a little kid at its side which could not have been more than a day or two old. While we were watching them, the African eagle stooped on the kid. As the eagle came close to the ground, the gerenuk leapt at it and seized a bunch of feathers out of its neck. The courage, and the timing, of the defence were superb and the eagle flew off without getting its claws on to its prey.

It is incidents like these which will, I hope, be remembered by my grandchildren all their lives. In fifty years time, when I hope my grandchildren will themselves be grandparents, I doubt whether there will be much wildlife left. The Kenyan government is doing its best to preserve what remains, but the pressures of a fast-growing population, poaching and excessive tourism, which I believe is beginning to harass the animals, are likely to diminish the stocks to a dangerous level. The position will be much the same in Uganda and Tanzania.

I have mentioned in this chapter the people who have mainly influenced my life. There is one other, my wife. We have been married for fifty years; she has rejoiced at my successes and sustained me in adversity and throughout that time she has been an unending source of strength. In Chapter 5 Jinny tells her side of the story and indicates how, among other responsibilities, a wife can help a busy professional man.

In recent years in the United Kingdom there has been a strong political desire to ensure that law and order prevail in our society. The decline in standards began in the 1960s and 1970s when the doctrine of the 'permissive society' became popular; it was openly sponsored by the Labour government. This was not the only reason. The miseries of inflation; unemployment; an increase in divorce and broken homes; mothers being out at work and not at home when their children return from school; poor teachers and bad schools, all played their part. As a result there has been an alarming increase in fraud, rape, drug addiction, crimes of violence, hooliganism at sports gatherings, child abuse and other crimes. At the present time the government is bringing in legislation to make it easier to bring criminals to book and to increase the penalties of wrong-doing. Legislation is no more than a palliative. The real solution, I believe, is to bring back discipline in the home and in the schools. Even if a campaign to this end began at once it would take a generation to achieve but, without it, law and order as we all want it to be will not be restored. Those of us who have been brought up with a good home background and to the strict discipline of a well-ordered school know only too well that it has affected the whole course of our lives and our behaviour in society. Unfortunately the media have power without responsibility and they do not always use it wisely. They could foster better discipline in the home and in schools if they abolished some of the wretched programmes and descriptions of crime and disorder which damage the minds of both young and old.

2.

Admission to Partnership
and the War Years 1934–45

When I became a partner in Cooper Brothers & Co in 1934, most of the partners were a good deal older than I was. The exception was John Pears. His father, Sydney Pears, was one of the first members of the staff who, in 1896, was promoted to partnership by the Cooper brothers. John joined the firm as an articled clerk in 1919 and was made a partner in 1926 at the age of 26. There was an age gap of nine years between us but we soon found that we shared the same views on most subjects. It was the beginning of a staunch and fertile friendship which lasted for nearly forty years. We both had some misgivings at that time about the way the firm was organised but we were too junior to make much impact. We had to wait until after the War before we could introduce the reforms we wanted.

One of the first clients I had to deal with was a man who told me that he was engaged to be married but, before the announcement was put in *The Times*, he wished to know a good deal more about his fiancée's financial affairs. He asked me to prepare a schedule of her debts and liabilities. He then intended to get them paid off by her parents, who were prominent in society, after which he would let the announcement go forward. The conditions he set did not seem a firm basis for future married bliss but I called on the lady and was enchanted by her. I did my best and rummaged through her writing desk but I am sure she concealed a good many of her debts; all those I did discover were duly liquidated by the girl's mother. The marriage did not last and the break-up provided banner headlines in the press for a day or two.

In those early years, I failed to detect two frauds which I

might have discovered. I investigated a small business in which a client wished to buy a share. It made temporary stands so that traders could exhibit their goods at exhibitions. I was glancing through the petty cash book when I noticed an entry 'cat's meat', costing a few shillings, which appeared once or twice each week. I said to the petty cashier that he seemed to have a very hungry cat, but he explained they were plagued with mice in the storeroom and it was necessary to have cats to keep the mice at bay. I learnt afterwards that there were neither cats nor mice, and this was merely a way in which the petty cashier supplemented his weekly wages, free of tax.

The other occasion was more serious. On one audit we had to work very late to finish the job by a fixed date. There were three or four of us working at about 11 pm, when the cashier put his head round the door and asked whether he could give us any help or perhaps drum up some refreshment for us. He hung about a bit, but I declined both offers. After he had gone, I remarked to my colleagues what agreeable behaviour this was and we were lucky to have such cooperative staff to deal with. If I had been more experienced and less trusting I would have said, 'That's strange. Why has he waited up to such a late hour? He must be frightened about something and he has come to see what we are doing.' The following year one of the audit staff noticed that a chemical eraser had been used to obliterate a handwritten entry in the ledger, but faint markings nevertheless remained. He was quick to follow this up, and found that the cashier had been 'teeming and lading', by purloining money from debtors and using subsequent remittances to cover his earlier defalcations. I think that if I had been more sceptical when he visited us late at night, we might have discovered earlier what was going on. He was convicted of theft in due course and went to prison.

In 1935 I went to Angola in West Africa to make a report on the financial position of the Benguela Railway which operated a railway line from the deep water harbour at Lobito Bay to the border with what was then the Belgian

Congo. The concept of this line of communication in Central Africa was due to Sir Robert Williams who hoped to be able to transport copper from the mines in Katanga and Northern Rhodesia to Lobito Bay for shipment worldwide. It was not an easy task for me because I spoke no Portuguese and few of the railway staff in Angola spoke English, with the result that a dialogue could only be carried on by frequent use of the dictionary.

At that time Angola did not have access to any of the conventional sources of power with result that the railway engines were fired by wood. There was a good deal of wood available locally but it was a formidable task to accumulate the large quantities which were needed and arrangements had to be made to set up plantations to provide supplies for the future.

I went up by train to the main centre of Nova Lisboa, which is about 150 miles from Lobito, and, after completing my work there, came back on an open ganger's car accompanied by the general manager of the railway. It was a good way to see the country and to become acquainted with the railway operation but it was a hot, slow and tedious process. In order to provide a change of diet we took a shot gun with us and from time to time picked off the francolin partridges which came to the railway line in the morning and evening to pick up grit for the benefit of their digestions. It is difficult enough to shoot partridges on the wing when standing on firm ground but it is a highly skilled operation when one is sitting on a conveyance which is moving at several miles an hour. Many of the partridges were unharmed but we managed to collect enough for our purposes. The general manager told me that, on his previous journey, a leopard who was playing 'last across' misjudged the speed of the ganger's car which cut off the last six inches of his tail.

Construction of the railway began in 1902, but it was not completed until 1928. It was well managed, but it needed a much greater volume of traffic to provide adequate revenues. In 1935 the mineral traffic from Katanga to Lobito

Bay was only 22,500 tons, and other traffic, 11,500 tons, which was nothing like the quantity which the founders of the railway had hoped for. This was partly because of the internal political squabbles which took place in Central Africa at that time and resulted in copper traffic being diverted from Lobito Bay to other and more expensive traffic routes. Thirty years later the traffic carried was much greater, and the comparable figures were 512,000 tons of mineral traffic and 177,000 tons of general traffic. I have not met anyone in recent years who can tell me what has happened to the railway or what part it is playing at present in the economic life of Angola. I believe the line has been completely disrupted by the internal war and chaos which has ravaged Angola for many years.

In 1937 an event occured which in a curious way repeated itself some forty-six years later and I relate the coincidence when writing about my experiences at the Bank of England. We were the auditors of an industrial client who was engaged in heavy electrical machinery and other engineering work. It got into serious financial difficulties and the firm was asked to help. I made a detailed investigation and report but the long and the short of it was that the company needed more money and its bankers refused to extend any further credit. The money needed for it to survive was about £300,000, which in those days was a large sum, and we could find no solution. This was worrying for other reasons; there was talk of war and rearmament and well found engineering companies could ill be spared.

In desperation I said to our then senior partner, Stuart Cooper, 'Let's go and talk to the Governor of the Bank of England.' At first he said that this was an absurd suggestion and asking to see Montagu Norman (later Lord Norman) was like asking for an interview with God, but he could not think of any better course of action and eventually we paid a visit to the Bank. I remember the day well because it was raining in sheets, my umbrella blew inside out on the way, and I arrived in a dishevelled state. We did not meet the Governor but saw the Deputy, B G Catterns who was courtesy itself.

He explained, in words which I myself often had to use many times over forty years later, that the Bank itself could not lend money nor could it influence the banks operating in the UK to extend credit beyond the limits they thought prudent. However, he asked us to leave the matter with him. The wheels then began to turn and, after some further meetings, additional money was found and the company survived and played its full part throughout the war years. Later it became a subsidiary of the Hawker Siddeley Group plc, a company of which I myself was a non-executive director from 1975 to 1981.

In 1938 a client of the firm in South Africa was anxious to obtain a listing of its shares on The Stock Exchange, London. The timing required early decisions and a journey by ship would have taken at least a fortnight. I therefore flew out to Johannesburg to make enquiries and obtain the necessary documentation. Commercial flying fifty years ago was only in its infancy, with the result that I went by flying boat, which was the only air route then available. We left from Southampton Water and stopped every four hours to refuel, arriving in Durban five days later. It was a tedious but otherwise agreeable form of transport. No night flying was permitted and we travelled at eight thousand feet or below and saw a good deal of the African continent.

We came down on the Nile for refuelling stops, but were not allowed to disembark until we got to Khartoum. At the first of these stops we watched Nile perch, about fifteen inches long, and, weighing, I suppose, about four or five pounds, swimming idly past the open cabin door. At each subsequent stop we therefore tied a bent pin to a bit of string and loaded it with delicacies. We frequently got a perch halfway out of the water but, alas, never into the cabin itself. In due course a listing of the shares in the company was obtained in London, but it lapsed during the Second World War.

In 1937 and 1938 the rumble of war became louder but many, of which I was one, found it difficult to believe that the nations of the world would in fact take the final step of declaring war and entering into a second carnage when the previous one, which had ended only twenty years earlier, was fresh in everybody's memory. My political judgements have never been reliable and the war started in 1939. When war breaks out in any country, a wave of patriotic fervour sweeps through the population, and I was caught up in the same hysteria. This is not merely a romantic idealism, because there is a much deeper feeling as well. Every citizen soon realises that his country and possibly even his own life are at stake, and he must get down to the job of doing his share in defeating the enemy. There is also a disagreeable stigma attaching to anyone who is thought to shirk the responsibility of 'doing his bit'. This spirit of everyone in the country working to a common purpose is one of the most profound emotions which grips the population in time of war. It creates a friendly and agreeable atmosphere and explains why tasks can be achieved which would be impossible under peace conditions. My name was put down for a commission in the Grenadier Guards largely, I think, through the good offices of D'Arcy Cooper and Viscount Trenchard.

'Boom' Trenchard and D'Arcy Cooper were great friends, and I met Trenchard from time to time in my uncle's company. D'Arcy advised him, in a private capacity, on some problems when he was appointed Commissioner of the Metropolitan Police in 1931, and in 1936 D'Arcy appointed Trenchard as Chairman of the United Africa Company Ltd which was a wholly owned subsidiary of Unilever.

Trenchard was a man of distinction in whatever circle he moved. He did not express himself easily, either orally or in writing, but he had the instinctive gift of knowing what the right course of action was, and the capacity to carry it through with relentless persistence. He started his life in the Army, but his greatest and most permanent achievement, attained by force of character and determination, was in building the Air Force in its formative years during and after the First World War when many prejudices and obstacles had to be overcome. He was made Marshall of the Royal Air Force in 1927. There is a fine statue of him in the Ministry of Defence gardens on the Embankment.

D'Arcy told me two stories about him. When he was commanding the West African Frontier Force in Nigeria in the early part of this century, he found that gambling, at cards and in other ways, was taking place among the officers, which was dangerous from the point of view of the welfare of the younger officers. He therefore issued an order that gambling was to stop. A short time later he walked into an officer's house after dinner and found gambling in progress. The officer reminded Trenchard that under the regulations a superior officer could not enter an officer's house without giving notice of his intention to visit him. Trenchard said he was aware of this, but that there was also a regulation that a commanding officer in his position had the right to repatriate any officer under his command. He added that there was a boat in the harbour sailing on the following day and he ordered the officer to leave on it.

The second story concerned his appointment as Commissioner of the Metropolitan Police. At that time there was disorder in the higher ranks of the police service and there had been allegations of bribery and corruption. The story goes that as soon as he was appointed Trenchard required all the senior officers to deliver their bank statements (called pass books in those days) to his office the following day. Each pass book was examined and unless the officer could explain every item of revenue credited to his account he was dismissed. Those who refused to comply were dismissed out of hand.

Twenty-seven years later I was engaged on an investigation where bribery was a possibility and I remembered this story. Bribery is difficult to detect and, with the same purpose in mind, I asked one of the officers of the concern whether he would allow me to inspect his bank statements. He agreed, but there was nothing untoward in any of them. The effect of this probing, however, was that he confessed that on one occasion he had been given an envelope full of bank notes. He took it home and kept it on the mantlepiece for two days, at the end of which he returned it. The hesitation in his decision, and the fact that he did not report the incident to his superiors, cast a shadow over his integrity.

Trenchard had a successful term of four years as Commissioner, and did a great deal to improve the standards and morale of the police force under his command. In later years I was friendly with both his sons. The elder one was a fellow officer in the Grenadiers, who was killed in the War in 1943, and his second son, now also dead, served Unilever for many years before entering politics in the Conservative cause.

Early in 1940 I was called to the regimental orderly room of the Grenadier Guards in Birdcage Walk to be interviewed by the Colonel of the regiment (referred to by tradition as the Lieutenant Colonel). He explained to me that I was the wrong age by one year. I was 29 but if I were 30 he could offer me a commission almost at once; at 29 there were problems. We had an eyeball to eyeball confrontation and I said, 'There is a war on; would it matter if my pen slipped?' 'Not at all,' he said, so I increased my age by one year.

Soon afterwards I was summoned to the training battalion at Victoria Barracks, Windsor and I remember that on a Wednesday in May 1940 I was working in the City and on the Thursday I was in uniform at Windsor as a second lieutenant completely unversed in any military knowledge. A commission in the Guards, without any previous training, was a startling and rewarding experience. Like most members of the general public, I had always had immense admiration for the Regiment, which was in no way diminished when I found myself part of it. The rigid, unswerving discipline, the attention to detail, and the determination that anything in which they engaged should be as good as human endeavour could make it, made a great impression which has remained with me ever since. Those factors create a respect for, and loyalty to, the Regiment, which is absorbed by those who have served in it, and it remains with them for the rest of their lives. Discipline and commitment are the creed of the Guards and it would do no harm if they were adopted more widely in civilian life. Advocates of a permissive society have not yet realised that those two qualities make for happiness, whereas their absence usually leads to discontent.

Huge difficulties were, of course, encountered in moving quickly from peace-time soldiering to a full war footing. There were large intakes of officers and guardsmen and a shortage of equipment but when, in due course, the Guards went into battle they distinguished themselves in accordance with their long tradition. Four others of the same age were commissioned at the same time as myself. Our initial training was ragged and not well organised and after a month or two we met together and decided to send a note to the commanding officer at Windsor saying that our training was not good enough. I cannot remember how we got the memorandum typed but it was duly delivered and it caused something of a stir. The first Guards were not accustomed to being told by their most inexperienced officers that their training was deficient. However, we were not reprimanded and the training courses improved. The equipment for training was woefully short. Apart from the rifle, the main weapon of the infantry was the Bren gun but very few specimens were available at Windsor. When we went on exercises a wooden mock-up of a Bren gun was carried as a symbol of what our armament ought to have been.

The five of us who joined at the same time were really out of place. The great majority of the young officers went straight from school to Sandhurst where they had a rigorous training. We were about ten years older and did not have that experience, with the result that we did not fit naturally into the normal regimental mould.

When I had been at Windsor for a few months I had a letter from the Military Secretary's department asking me to confirm my age by sending a copy of my birth certificate. I explained the position to the battalion adjutant but he washed his hands of the problem and said I must find a way out of it myself. I did not think that it would help matters, or improve my relations with the Lieutenant Colonel, by recounting my conversation with him. I finally concocted a careful reply explaining the problems of tracing birth certificates in South Africa issued some thirty years earlier particularly if, as I hinted, they were issued at all at that time. I heard no more.

The task of training new recruits quickly (men and officers) was immense. A large proportion of the young guardsmen had been brought up in big cities and had little or no acquaintance with the countryside. Their understanding of the cover offered by trees and vegetation and the use of ground was virtually nil. I remember that on one occasion, after the appropriate lecture, a section of eight men were given the task under the platoon sergeant of seeing how close they could approach the Copper Horse in Windsor Great Park (where the instructing officers were based) without being observed. Soon after the exercise began, we saw eight large green bushes, each more or less concealing a guardsman, moving in open order at a steady pace though open country towards the Copper Horse. Military precision was well maintained and each bush was a uniform ten paces from its neighbour. They would have provided a perfect target for any hostile marksman. What was even more astonishing was the sergeant's chagrin when it was pointed out to him that this was not what was meant by the use of cover and camouflage, and that a more subtle approach was needed.

Like all young officers, I had to serve my turn as an officer in charge of the guard which was always maintained at Windsor Castle. Accompanied by a non-commissioned officer and two guardsmen, I had to inspect the sentries on duty at least once every night between 23.00 hours and dawn. For this purpose we were not allowed to patrol the terrace on one side of the Castle for fear of waking the two Princesses (Elizabeth and Margaret) who slept in that area. We were, therefore, required to make a detour through the gardens to get to the next sentry point. It was assumed, I

suppose, that marauders with evil intent who wished to
enter the Castle would be equally careful to avoid disturbing
the Princesses' slumbers.

On one such inspection I thought I would test the
initiative of one of the guardsmen. I said, 'Assume you
suddenly saw a lot of German parachutists dropping from
the skies in the grounds out there (with a lofty wave of the
arm), intent on attacking the Castle. What would you do?'
There was a long pause and eventually the guardsman said,
'Send for a policeman'. This extraordinary reply made me
wonder how he would even alert the guardsman in the next
sentry box, let alone an unarmed policeman or the guard
itself, both of whom were half a mile away. I wrote a report
to the commanding officer at the barracks, suggesting that
some system of intercommunication between the guard
points, and with the rest of the guard, might be helpful in
case of an emergency. The point was taken up at once, and
thereafter a whistle was hung on a peg in each sentry box
which the guardsman could blow if he felt endangered.
Happily I do not think that this new technology was ever put
to the test because the Castle guard never had to face the
problem of protecting the sovereign or his family from
attack, either by prowlers or the enemy.

Over forty years later a man did find his way one night
into the Queen's bedroom at Buckingham Palace without
being noticed. Fortunately he was docile and no great
harm resulted, except to the reputation of the security
arrangements in and outside the Palace.

During part of my time at Windsor I was put in charge of
training the young officers in fieldcraft. They arrived
periodically, in squads of about fifteen, after completing
their training course at Sandhurst. In one of these squads
there were two young gentlemen who I thought were idle
and spineless, and in my formal report I said that I did not
think they would ever make satisfactory Grenadier officers
The Lieutenant Colonel came down from London and said
that he had more experience in judging the young entry than
I had, and he proposed to ignore my advice. Both men had

very good wars in the regiment and one of them won the Military Cross in Italy.

My memory is hazy about dates in those hectic years but I think I remained at Windsor until late 1941. I was then posted to a Guards battalion which was stationed in Scotland and thence to the headquarters of the Command where I worked on the staff.

In 1942 I was recruited, and I do not know how or why, to join the Special Operations Executive (SOE), which was a special branch of the services engaged in every form of undercover work, including the organisation of resistance in occupied territories. At the beginning of the war SOE got off to a bad start and it was despised by the regular services as a ragged collection of irregulars, who were engaged in what was rather contemptuously described as 'cloak and dagger stuff'. In November 1940 Major General Sir Colin Gubbins DSO took command, and he brought it to an efficient force with great achievements to its credit.

The staff recruited to SOE were a mixed bag and a few of them not of high quality. The bulk of them, however, comprised men and women with considerable talents, many of whom were exceptional in courage and initiative. The people who were dropped behind the lines in enemy territory (usually by air, but sometimes by sea) knew very well that if they were detected, or their security was 'blown' by others, they would almost certainly be shot and possibly tortured first. SOE operated in many theatres of war, but it reached its zenith just before and after the landings in Europe in 1944. The network of resistance groups which had been organised behind the enemy lines provided massive help to the invading allied forces, by arson and sabotage and the disruption of enemy lines of communication. The intelligence they were able to provide was invaluable. On joining SOE I was promoted to major and went, as one of a special mission, to New York to organise the ordering and delivery of special equipment, particularly radio and electrical goods which were needed for the undercover operations of SOE.

When Churchill came to power in 1940 he declared that we had only one objective in view, and that was victory over Germany. Although everyone in the country was behind him and determined to win the war whatever the cost, some felt that a total capitulation by the enemy might not be attained and some form of armistice might eventually be arranged. The Japanese attacked the American fleet in Pearl Harbor on 7 December 1941 and America declared war immediately. I was in London in a room full of people when the details of the attack were announced. At the end of it there was total silence for some seconds; then a young girl, bending over her typewriter, said in a loud, clear, voice, 'That makes victory certain.' I think it reflected the mood of everyone in Britain from that time forward. A year or two later Roosevelt coined the phrase 'unconditional surrender'.

America opened my eyes to an entirely new world and I realised what a narrow life I had hitherto led. When I arrived there in 1942, America had been a belligerent for only a few months, but the commitment to victory was complete. On a personal basis, we were at all times treated as friends and allies, and in both social and military spheres the American people were generous and welcoming to anyone in the uniform of the British forces. Their hospitality was at times overwhelming. Like Britain in 1939, they were still coping with some of the problems which confront any country suddenly faced with total war, and although they were altogether helpful in spirit, the sense of urgency which by that time was ingrained in everyone in Britain had not yet spread across the Atlantic.

Merely by way of example, we needed one particular piece of equipment urgently. This was the inflammatory pencil. It was about the same size and shape as a lead pencil and the outer skin was made of soft metal. When the metal was squeezed it brought chemicals together which, after a time (varying from one hour to several hours depending on the type) gave out an intense flame. These were distributed wherever arson could help the war effort. They were issued in neutral ports so that they could be dropped into the holds of ships which were carrying goods and equipment to Germany. They were also used for starting fires in warehouses and buildings. We had to wait months for this relatively simple piece of equipment but, when supplies did come forward, they were in such immense quantities that we did not know what to do with them. I returned to SOE in London in June 1943.

John Pears was too old for active service and was appointed as Principal Controller of Costs at the Ministry of Supply where his main responsibility was the supervision of costs of government contracts. One of the other activities of the Ministry of Supply was the control and direction of the Royal Ordnance Factories which made guns, explosives and munitions of all sorts for the three Services. There were some forty-four factories in all parts of the country employing between 300,000 and 400,000. The accounts of the ordnance factories were in chaos which was a severe impediment to John Pears in his work and he eventually suggested in the corridors of power that I should be seconded from the army to put some order into their accounting processes. After some haggling with the War Office I went to the Ministry of Supply in September 1943 as an 'adviser' to the ordnance factories, but I realised within the first week that this was a hopeless task. Either I must have executive authority or I was wasting my time.

A curious interview took place with the Deputy Secretary of the Ministry of Supply. I explained the chaos which I had found. The Deputy Secretary thought I would wish to stay as 'adviser' and never dreamed that anyone would volunteer to take on the responsibility of restoring order. He asked very tentatively, and without much conviction in his voice, whether I thought it could be put right with the limited resources of trained manpower available in war time. I said yes I thought it could and I would like to be given the opportunity to try and do so. He was taken aback but shortly afterwards I was appointed Director of Factories (Accounts) with the necessary authority. The staff in the factories for whom I had functional responsibility on accounting matters numbered about 10,000. The ordnance factories in peace time were, I think, only three in number, the main one being at Woolwich. When war was imminent, the other forty-one factories were established at great speed and with inadequate trained administrative staff or clear instructions on accounting or financial matters. The emphasis was on the engineering and technical aspects and the high quality of munitions was never, as far as I know, seriously criticised; but the internal administration was awful. Instead of using the normal double-entry system of bookkeeping which has been routine for scores of years, most of the factories were on 'single entry' and accountants will know by this description how inefficient they were and how loose the control was.

The next few months were the most hectic I have ever spent. I worked very hard and for long hours at a great pace. Under war conditions one could do things which would be impossible in peace time and I exploited the situation to the full. It was necessary to overcome a crisis. First, I visited most, if not all, the factories. I took an exercise book with me and noted down everything that seemed to need attention. I then came back to London and wrote a manual of instruction. There were four aspects to be dealt with: the control of cash, of stores, of wages and of costings. I tackled them one by one. Cash was the first priority. From a given date I ordered all the factories to suspend all their existing cash records and to start afresh on the basis of the manual of instruction on cash. They were not permitted to buy or use any stationery or books except those specified in the manual. Returns had to be submitted to me monthly and if any return was so much as a day late I got on to the telephone and demanded an immediate explanation. If there was any hitch I sent one of my staff in London to the factory to clear up the trouble and report who was responsible for the breakdown. In due course I dealt with stores and wages in the same way and at the end made some radical changes in the costing procedures.

I also demanded that all offices should at once be cleaned

up and made scrupulously tidy. All papers were to be properly filed; desks were to be cleared every night; no books, papers or parcels were to be stored on top of filing cabinets; desks were to be properly aligned and not set out higgledy-piggledy. The stores were a major problem, but here again I insisted on proper storage in bins and racks and a bin card system; this was a huge task. In those days the uniform of a Grenadier officer, if not in battle dress, included a handsome blue forage cap, leather gloves and a walking stick. I toured the factories, impeccably turned out, to satisfy myself that the manuals were being properly observed. I tapped the floor with my stick for emphasis or used it to point out anything I did not like. The accounting staff did not know what to make of this; it was a new experience for them (and for me) but they responded to the disciplines imposed upon them. The insistence on cleanliness and tidiness eventually became something of a cult in the factories and I am sure it improved efficiency and stimulated an orderly approach to work by the staff. I remember my astonishment one day when, in the middle of the Blitz, I went on a visit to Woolwich and found a man solemnly painting white lines on the floor of one of the large offices so that all the desks in the room could be aligned precisely.

I was also tough with the staff. Anybody who did not pull his weight was got rid of by some means or other and I promoted everyone who seemed capable of doing the job and complying strictly with the manuals. This led to a complaint by the Unions who felt that I was not giving proper regard to age and period of service. A meeting was arranged to discuss the complaints and the Unions put forward specific cases which they believed had been wrongly dealt with. I knew all the cases intimately and was able to give convincing reasons for any action taken. I was asked about a cashier at one of the factories who controlled several staff and why he had been demoted to a dead-end job on his own. I said, 'Because he pinches the bottoms of the girls in his office'. This virtually closed the meeting and I did not have any further complaints.

One of the edicts I issued was that all old records were to be burnt. This was done in order to clean up the offices which were overcrowded and untidy and to make better use of the limited space available. Woolwich put up a stout resistance to this and I went down to see the situation on the spot. They pointed to row upon row of old files stacked from floor to ceiling which they said were an essential part of the history of Woolwich and urged that these records, going back scores of years, should be retained at all costs. I insisted on destruction. A few days later I was told that, when they collected the files to put them in the incinerator, they found that there was nothing there but the fronts of the files. Mice had eaten the rest.

I spent about ten months on the job altogether and during that time reduced the staff employed in the factories on financial records by about nine hundred. The accounts, though primitive, were by then in good shape and the monthly returns were up to date. In that period I learnt more about practical accounting and dealing with people than I have learnt before or since, and it stood me in good stead in later years.

While at SOE in the early part of 1943 I had the opportunity to see the plans for Overlord and knew the dates when the landings in France by the Allied forces were scheduled to take place. I thought it was time to get back to the regiment and in the spring of 1944 I applied to be returned to normal duty. However, that did not last long. Towards the end of 1944 the war in the Mediterranean was virtually at an end. SOE had a substantial organisation based in Cairo called Force 133 from which they controlled the undercover and resistance operations in Greece and the Balkans. SOE was anxious to close this down and send the staff and suitable equipment to other theatres of war. SOE applied for me to be returned to them for this cleaning-up operation. I was promoted to the rank of full colonel and despatched to Cairo. The SOE operations in Cairo were curious. There was a large staff but there were more officers than men and there was a motley collection of equipment in some quantity. I took over from a brigadier who before being put in charge of the SOE had been on the staff of the Eighth Army. He was engagingly frank about his change of post. When General Montgomery took command in the Middle East he sent for the brigadier on the second day and said, 'You're too old. I want you to leave at once', which he did. That was the beginning and the end of the interview.

I set about Force 133 in the Middle East with the same enthusiasm as I had attacked the ordnance factories. Within two or three months I had despatched all the personnel to their new postings and had sold or otherwise got rid of the equipment including some Greek caiques which had been an essential part of the undercover operations. I was concerned, however, about the Greek patriots who had helped Force 133 loyally and to great effect during the difficult years when the Germans were in occupation in Greece. Many of them had died or been killed and there was the problem of supporting their families. So in February 1945 I flew back to London for two days. I saw John Venner, the chief finance officer of SOE, a chartered accountant who became a personal friend and who, at the time of joining the forces, was a partner in Edward Moore & Co. He was quick and efficient. We went to the Treasury together and asked for £200,000 out of secret funds to support, or ease the burdens of, the families of any accredited member of the Greek resistance movement. £200,000 does not sound a large sum but in 1945 it was a substantial amount. It was granted at once and was paid into a joint account in a bank in the West End of London in the names of John Venner and myself. We were never asked to account to anyone for the use and application of these funds but meticulous accounts were, of course, kept.

I went back to Cairo and organised a committee of four prominent Greek citizens in Athens, including the Archbishop, who could advise us about the genuine cases where help was needed. The chief member of this committee was John Pelthakis who had himself been the leader of the Greek resistance movement throughout the war. I had great respect for him – not only for his achievements but his powers of leadership. I was told at the time, and had no reason to disbelieve it, that on one night he himself sank or disabled eleven enemy ships in Piraeus harbour. This was achieved by paddling round under cover of darkness and attaching limpet mines which in two or three hours exploded and blew holes in the steel hulls. He knew no English when war broke out but taught himself by listening every night to the BBC news. When I first met him in 1945 he spoke and wrote English fluently.

For many years John Venner and I (and, after he died, I alone) disbursed this fund and its accruing interest. We helped four hundred families. Sometimes we paid for children's education and in one or two cases brought students to London; we bought small businesses or gave other assistance which eased difficulties. Apart from the merits of the operation this helped Anglo–Greek relations. After sixteen years, however, the task was completed and in 1961 I went out to the British Embassy in Athens and formally brought the fund to an end. I presented gold watches to the members of the committee who had been particularly active. The final ceremony was an emotional event for all of us who took part.

There was about £11,000 left of the original sum of £200,000 but its disposal was extremely difficult. It seems that secret funds have to be used for that purpose and they cannot be brought back into the national finances. It took well over a year to find a solution. I had correspondence and interviews with Burke Trend (later Lord Trend) at the Treasury in order to find a solution. Eventually we set up a discretionary trust in Athens to dispose of the money.

Having disbanded Force 133 I came back to London in March 1945 and then abandoned army uniform and became Controller of Building Materials at the Ministry of Works. There was, of course, a shortage of building materials for housing and the vast rehabilitation necessary to repair the ravages of German bombing. The task was to stimulate supplies of all building materials; to give financial help if needed; and, in some cases, to control prices.

The Minister of Works was Duncan Sandys (later Lord Duncan-Sandys) and the permanent secretary was Sir Percival Robinson. One event caused much trouble. The cement industry had an unequivocal agreement with the ministry (entered into before I joined) that if the price of coal was to rise, the price of cement would be adjusted appropriately. This took place and I authorised an increase in the price of cement, stipulating that it would not take place until the cement manufacturers had used up their existing stocks of coal. Looking back, I should have warned the minister that the rise was to take place, but I did not do so because the increase seemed to me to be inevitable and only a matter of routine.

The increase was sixpence a ton, which in terms of the present value of money does not seem important, but it was significant at that time. When it was announced there was an outburst in the press and I was summoned, on a Saturday morning, to see the minister and the permanent secretary. The minister felt that he had lost face and the issue rumbled on for a few days and other departments were consulted. One of the people drawn into the mêlée was Harold Wilson (later Lord Wilson of Rievaulx) who was not then an MP, but was working for the government as a temporary civil servant. Over twenty years later I attended a function at Downing Street when Harold Wilson was prime minister and I was introduced to him. Without a moment's hesitation, he said, 'Do you remember the sixpence a ton on cement?' which impressed me as a remarkable feat of memory for a person carrying his responsibilities.

I stayed on at the Ministry of Works for a few months, but found Percival Robinson impossible to work with. I was, therefore, glad when later in 1945 Sir William Douglas, the permanent secretary at the Ministry of Health, asked me to join his department on a special assignment of three months to advice on housing production. Percival Robinson raised a great shout about this, but I cannot imagine why, as he must have been as glad to see the back of me as I was to be rid of him. A few months later I was pleased to hear that he was displaced as permanent secretary and given other employment.

Housing was, of course, one of the many urgent needs as the War came to a close. The appointment was limited to three months because I wanted to get back to civilian life at the beginning of 1946. Aneurin Bevan was the minister in charge. He was, as we all know, Left in his political views. The deputy secretary was in equal measure to the Right, but they got on splendidly together. On the occasions when I had to see Bevan I also found him easy to work with. As the head of the Department he was clear and definite in his views and decisions and had an engaging sense of humour. At the Ministry of Health I worked long hours but did not achieve anything which is worth recording. The appointments at both government departments were unpaid. On 1 January 1946 I left to continue in practice as a partner in Cooper Brothers & Co.

I learnt more in the five years of the War than in any other period of my life. I was 36 when the conflict ended and I had had experience in a number of different ways. The two most lasting effects were first, an understanding of adminis-tration, both large and small, and especially the pitfalls to be avoided. Second, it made me much more sensitive in dealing with people. I learnt the hard way, that in practically every situation it takes perhaps 2 or 3 per cent of one's time to find the solution and the remaining 97 or 98 per cent has to be spent in convincing other people what needs to done and trying to get some action.

Two other lessons were borne in on me which have helped to save many hours of what would otherwise be wasted time. Time was short in the war years and if I could not understand a document at the first reading I came to the conclusion that it was not me that was in the wrong but the document. Whenever I have been in a position to do so I have therefore always sent back (sometimes with asperity) any piece of writing which is not clear; and I try to test my own written work, even difficult technical material, by asking myself whether a reader will understand what I mean after he has read it once. For much the same reasons I believe that any piece of writing of any length should always end (or begin) with a summary of the writer's conclusions; I become impatient and am inclined to ignore any document which does not do so. These simple precepts have saved many hours of otherwise wasted effort.

In 1946 I was made a CBE for my work during the War.

3.

The Post-War Development of
Cooper Brothers and Company 1946–75

I do not propose to write a history of Cooper Brothers & Co or, as it is now called, Coopers & Lybrand. I wrote a history of the first hundred years from 1854 to 1954 and an addendum was written by others in 1979 at the end of 125 years. I merely recount some of the events in its history and development with which I was particularly concerned. In later chapters I describe some of the special assignments and appointments which arose as a result of being a partner in the firm.

The strength of the firm was built on the integrity and competence of the four brothers Cooper – William, Arthur, Francis (my grandfather) and Ernest. At the outbreak of the First World War three of the brothers were dead and only Ernest remained, but by their industry and integrity they had built up a good and successful practice with many important clients. It was said by the staff in the firm that the principle on which they carried on business was that the highest form of praise was the absence of a complaint. I am sometimes accused of having inherited this mode of life, but it is not wholly true. The First World War denuded the firm of almost all its staff and the problem was to keep it going. When D'Arcy Cooper came back from the war in 1919 he began to resuscitate the firm and was making substantial progress when he joined Lever Brothers Ltd as vice chairman in 1923. From 1923 to the beginning of the Second World War in 1939 the firm stagnated in some degree and it fell behind the other firms of equivalent size and standing. John Pears was made a partner in 1926 and was beginning to make his mark but he could not bring about on his own the radical changes which were needed. The firm was beginning to make progress when the Second World War broke out and then again it was a question of survival; the great majority of the staff left to join the forces or undertake the work to which they were directed by the government.

John Pears had returned to full practice in the latter part of 1945 and I went back on 1 January 1946. We were full of enthusiasm, enjoyed good health, and had common interests; we agreed that our purpose was to restore morale and ensure that the firm played its full part in the profession. We wanted to expand both at home and overseas, to increase the clientele and to build an international organisation which would hold its own with the other international firms then in existence. We believed that there was much to be done to bring the firm's technical work up to date and that the pay and conditions of the staff needed overhaul. We worked together on this task for the next twenty-five years. One of the problems was the then senior partner, Stuart Ranson Cooper, son of Ernest Cooper. He had a clear brain and could express himself lucidly in speech and writing but he was not convinced that expansion on the scale we had in mind was necessary or desirable. His health was patchy and he was not willing to put into the firm the work and energy it needed. After some difficult meetings in 1946, which the senior partners left to John and me to handle, he agreed to retire. John was then made senior partner in his place and the way was clear for the reforms we wanted to introduce.

After Stuart Cooper retired, John made a generous gesture to me. He said that he and I would work together as equals in the partnership and that we would run it together. He was nine years senior to me and could be expected to take a larger share of the profits. Also he could have insisted on maintaining that he was the senior partner in all decisions. He was, of course, the senior partner in fact and he presided over the partners' meetings until the late 1960s, but his willingness, which he loyally observed, to treat me in all respects on an equal footing made a great impression upon me and I think it was at the heart of our success together. We trusted each other implicitly and would accept decisions made when one or other of us was overseas without question. Neither of us, operating alone, could have achieved the development of the firm which took place in the post-war years, but, together, we formed a very strong team.

In the last few years of his life John was upset that his work was not recognised by any form of public award. He fully deserved it and was, I think, unfairly treated. I know that his name was put forward for a knighthood for his work in the War at the Ministry of Supply but at some point it was blocked, possibly because he was forthright and outspoken in his work and comments at the Ministry, and this must have upset somebody who had the power of veto. Later on, with others, I tried hard to ensure that his work in the profession and in the public sector was properly recognised, but we were not successful.

One of the first tasks I undertook after the War was to write a manual for use in the firm. I had learnt the success this could achieve as a result of my experience in the ordnance factories during the War. As the years went by the manual was improved regularly and frequently and it was the basis on which all our work and administration was subsequently based. It was a condition of every office which was opened anywhere in the world that (subject to local conditions) it should conduct its affairs and practice on the basis of the manual.

The manual was particularly important because of the major changes pending in company law which influenced the work of the profession in the post-war years. A new Companies Act came into force in 1948 following the report made by the Cohen Company Law Amendment Committee. It made not only consolidated accounts compulsory but it led to another profound effect in the presentation of the accounts of limited companies and the auditor's report. Prior to 1948 the law had required that the accounts should be 'true and correct', a term which was interpreted in many ways. A set of accounts can be technically true and correct but may totally fail to present a fair picture of the company's financial position. Before the 1948 Act came into force it was not unusual for accountants to say, 'Well, it is on the right side'. In short, provided that the accounts as presented to shareholders and the public showed a worse position than was in fact the case they could be accepted. For example, if stock was undervalued or a provision for debts was excessive, this was not thought to be a serious blemish on the presentation of the accounts because the true position was better than that shown. The 1948 Act changed the whole situation. It required that the accounts should be 'true and fair'. This meant that the doctrine of 'correctness' or 'it is on the right side' went out of the window. In effect substance took precedence over form. Companies and their auditors took a little time to adjust to this concept but it is now an accepted doctrine. In America and in some other countries the words used in the audit report are 'fairly present' which comes to the same thing. The case law decisions which have taken place throughout the world in the last forty years on the proper presentation of accounts have endorsed this doctrine of true and fair and made it clear that it virtually overrides other considerations.

The war-time experiences which John Pears and I had undergone convinced us that there was a new field for development in the profession. We found that many people, under the stress of the new conditions engendered by the War, wanted skilled and independent advice on planning, organisation and administration and we were determined to study this in depth when we got back into the profession. Our new project got off the ground slowly. There was much to do in our traditional fields and in the early post-war years we were still suffering from every sort of shortage, not least of skilled staff. Gradually, however, the venture took shape and this led to the formation of an ancillary activity – management consultancy. Success in this field means harnessing different professional skills besides accountants – engineers, information technology, transport, manu-facturing, the distributive industries and others. All these had to be coordinated under specialised management and in 1962 we therefore set up a separate subsidiary undertaking called Coopers & Lybrand Associates which has prospered and is able to service clients in many specialised fields of consultancy work.

In the immediate post-war years the firm began to get a great deal of new work despite the difficulties of finding staff. One of our first steps overseas was to enlarge our interests in Canada. In 1948, following an introduction to George Currie of Macdonald Currie & Co, one of the leading Canadian firms, John Pears went to Montreal and we began an association in Canada which has been of lasting benefit. We also opened offices in the provinces in the United Kingdom and in Europe, Australia, East Africa, Northern and Southern Rhodesia, Nyasaland, New Zealand, West Africa and the Congo. This was done by sending parners and staff to open a practice or by amalgamating with local practitioners who were willing to adopt our name and to be bound by the manual and the rigid conditions which we imposed in our partnership agreements.

John and I travelled abroad extensively, not only for the purpose of opening new outlets but as 'follow up' to ensure that each practice overseas was running in the way which we thought necessary. John reckoned that after the War he travelled over a million miles on the firm's business and I cannot think that I did any less. It was very hard work. It meant being away from home for long and short periods and, as may be expected, things did not always run smoothly. Problems were often encountered. The need to maintain quality was always with us and this is particularly difficult in some areas of the world where there is a shortage of well-trained and experienced accountants.

On these visits abroad I was often asked to make speeches on professional topics to the staff of the firm, or to the members of the profession and students. I was once asked to address the students in Perth, Australia, and as we were going into dinner the chairman asked me what I was going to talk about but, when I told him, his comment was so

scathing that I had to extemporise with much lighter
material than I intended. I mention this incident in another
context on page 57.

These visits abroad after the War had other uses. I was an
admirer of Geoffrey Heyworth (later Lord Heyworth) who
succeeded D'Arcy Cooper as chairman of Unilever in 1941
and I had the warmest admiration for him. After the War,
whenever I was travelling the world on the firm's business, I
always called in to see the local Unilever organisation and
asked to be shown over the factories which had been
established in the territory. Geoffrey expected me always to
call on him as soon as I got back and to give him my
impressions. He was, of course, very well informed but he
liked to get an impartial and independent view. At these
meetings we also discussed many different subjects which
was always invigorating and I gained much from the wide
range of his knowledge.

He told me that one of his many tasks was to watch
subordinate managers making mistakes but *not to interfere*
otherwise they would not learn by their mistakes. His job
was to provide the judgement required to follow this policy
and decide when to intervene, if intervention became
imperative.

The way in which he first joined the Lever organisation is
not without interest. He was educated at the Academy in the
small town of Dollar in Scotland, where he was captain of
the rugger fifteen, captain of cricket and, in his closing year,
the best scholar in the school. At the age of 18 his future had
to be settled. His widowed mother had seen the rise of
William Hesketh Lever, who had set the world talking with
his model community at Port Sunlight and his expanding
industrial enterprises. Mrs Heyworth decided to journey
south to ask this superman for a job for her boy. As she had
no appointment and no letter of introduction, she was
brusquely told at the Liverpool offices of Lever Brothers that
the chairman was not available. Calmly, she sat down to
wait and, when he appeared, put her request in typical
Yorkshire directness. The man who terrorised his staff with

his abruptness listened. His comment was, 'If your son is anything like you, he'll do.' He did – in 1912 he started as a clerk in the accounts department and developed into one of the finest administrators of his generation.

During these hectic years in public practice I made a great many other friends among clients for whom the firm carried out professional work and there is space to mention only one or two. One of these was Harry Pilkington (later Lord Pilkington). The family business of glass makers, Pilkington Brothers Ltd, was started in St Helens in Lancashire in 1826 and it was still a private company when I first knew it. Harry joined the firm in 1927, became chairman in 1949 and led it for the ensuing twenty-four years during which it became a great international group. In industrial affairs he had the clearest financial mind that I have ever encountered and a remarkable power to grasp and interpret figures. He was one of the first to realise the damaging effects of inflation so that, in his own business, progress was measured in current values and not on historical costs; this was one of the secrets of its success. In private life he was a shy man with simple tastes and his style of living was unostentatious and, at times, austere. During the War when petrol was short he went about on a bicycle and continued to do so for many years afterwards. He never wore an overcoat. At that time I was living at Merstham in Surrey, twenty miles from London, and one winter's evening there was a ring at the front door. There was Harry who had bicycled down on chance. He had supper with us but could not be persuaded to stay the night and pedalled off back to London. Later, on an evening in the summer, I saw him bicycling down Pall Mall on his way to a banquet in full evening dress with his black coat tails streaming out behind him like a swallow in flight.

Another staunch friend was Louis Franck. He was a Belgian citizen by birth but was awarded a CBE for his services in the British army during the War. We met during the War and when peace was restored he asked me to advise him about the future of the merchant banking house Samuel

Montagu & Co which he ran in the City in conjunction with a loyal friend and partner, David Keswick. At that time it was a partnership but it was turned into a private limited company and prospered exceedingly.

Louis was a keen sailor and a generous host. He represented Belgium in the Olympics after the War and later built a motor cruiser in which every detail was planned with meticulous care for the comfort of the passengers and the crew. My wife and I have enjoyed many happy trips with him and his wife in the Mediterranean. Early in the 1980s he asked me whether I thought he could make a fund available for scholarships in the City. After I had taken the advice of the then Governor of the Bank of England on his behalf, Louis set up a trust fund of a substantial amount to provide scholarships for young people in the City who showed promise, in order that they could obtain experience abroad, particularly in universities overseas. The intention was that they should in due course return to the City and, in the years to come, provide leadership in the way in which he himself had done. These grants have continued ever since and are serving the purpose which he had in mind. Louis died in 1988 and, at a dinner for past scholars held in London in 1989, a warm debt of gratitude was expressed on behalf of them all.

Shortly after the War we absorbed the practice of a firm of chartered accountants in the provinces. They had, among many other clients, a large and successful engineering group with a number of subsidiaries. The chairman had established a high reputation as an industrialist and in other ways, but he was arrogant and had bullied the predecessor firm for some years previously. The audits which took place after the merger gave rise to difficulties in some of the subsidiaries, particularly as regards stock valuation, and we asked for amendments to be made to the accounts to avoid qualifications in our audit reports. A meeting with the chairman and executive directors was held later in the year to settle the accounts of the parent company but I was asked to see the chairman privately for five minutes beforehand.

He came straight to the point and said, 'I want you to resign as auditors.' I asked why and he said, 'Because I wish it.' I said I would not. The scheduled meeting then began in a strained atmosphere.

A few days later a meeting of the full board took place. While some of the directors and I were waiting in the ante-room before the meeting, a fearful clanging broke out from engineering work which was taking place outside. The managing director turned to me and to the amusement of his fellow directors said, 'For whom the bell tolls.' I was enraged at being made fun of but could not think of a suitable reply; it hardened my resolve for the meeting which was about to begin. At the board meeting I again refused to resign. I was then told that the board would put forward a resolution at the annual general meeting to have us replaced by other auditors. Between the two meetings I had consulted the President of our Institute about the ethical problem and Sir David Maxwell-Fyfe QC about the legal issues. I therefore said that I would write a letter to the shareholders and to The Stock Exchange, London and I wished a copy of the letter to be sent to every shareholder with the notice convening the general meeting. The letter was approved by counsel and was strictly factual but forthright in its terms. It explained that the reason for requiring our resignation had arisen because of the stand we had taken on certain issues affecting the true and fair view of the group accounts.

When the board received the letter they began to waver and sent two of their non-executive directors (who were both well known and respected in the City) to see John Pears and me to try and persuade us by soft language to resign lest the ensuing fracas damage our reputation, or so they averred. We regarded it as a fundamental matter of principle and refused point blank and also pointed out that the contretemps was more likely to damage their company than us. The board then gave way and we continued as auditors. The chairman died a year or two later which eased the situation.

I was often asked to negotiate, on behalf of clients,

purchases and sales of shares in private companies or, at times, a complete business. It was my practice before going into any negotiation for a sale to make up my mind on two figures: (1) the lowest I would accept; and (2) the figure which I thought was a good price with which the owner should be well satisfied. Anything over that was a luxury or bonus figure which it would be nice to obtain if my powers of persuasion were equal to the task.

In one such negotiation involving a parcel of shares, my opponent was a partner in one of the other large accounting firms. I forget the precise figures now but they were something of the order of: (1) £36 million (2) £38 million. After much haggling we got as far as £38 million, but I tried to raise the figure by an extra £1 million. I was getting nowhere when my opponent said, 'Will you toss for it?' I said 'Yes, sudden death.' I lost. I have never recounted this story to anyone before because it would not be helpful if my clients thought I gambled a possible £1 million of their money on the spin of a coin and I imagine my opponent has been equally reticent for the same reason. I felt no remorse; I had settled a good price, with which the clients were well content, and the chances of improving it seemed remote. A lucky spin of the coin would have been an unexpected bonus.

John Pears was elected to the Council of the Institute of Chartered Accountants in England and Wales in 1946 and took a considerable part in its affairs. He became President in the year 1960. I also began to take a great interest in Institute affairs and was elected to the Council in 1956 and was made President for the year 1966. In accordance with tradition, I made a short speech when I was elected indicating what I hoped to achieve in my year of office. I had five points; three were of a topical nature at that time and do not warrant repetition, but the other two were of long-term importance. I said that I had been invited, as President, to visit Canada and America to attend meetings of the Institutes in those countries and added: 'I have had the feeling for a long time that our relations with those Institutes

were very friendly but somewhat remote and, with the
Council's approval, I shall see whether I can perhaps get
them on to a more intimate basis.'

I prepared this statement carefully beforehand. My private
but unstated ambition at that stage was to make it, as I think
it turned to to be, a turning point in the history of the
accountancy profession. The United Kingdom, America and
Canada were the three most important countries at that time
in the world of accountancy, but there was very little
dialogue between them. No attempt had been made to bring
them closer together to advance the interests of the
profession as a whole or to get a common approach to
accountancy and audit problems. The Canadian institute
was closer to the American institute than we were because
of their geographical position but each of the three pursued
its own policies without reference or collaboration with the
other two. I hoped to change this. All I wanted at that stage
was the Council's approval to the idea, which was readily
given. This was the beginning of the Accountants
International Study Group and the formation of the
International Accounting Standards Committee which are
described in Chapter 6. These moves began to foster
dialogue and collaboration on a worldwide international
basis. It tilled the soil for the later planting and growth of the
International Federation of Accountants which finally came
into being in 1977.

The second point was stated in this way:

And the fifth and last thing is one which is very dear to my
heart. Our Institute is really founded basically on
auditing; entirely new techniques have now been forced
on us by the advent of computers, and the requirements of
the Stock Exchange, and by the new Companies Bill
which is likely to be published in a few months' time and
which will impose even more rigorous standards. I
suspect that some members of the Council have doubts
whether our own recommendations to our members are as

widely known or recognised as we would wish; I feel very strongly that we should mount a massive attack on this subject to see whether we can revivify the new techniques of auditing that this Council itself has recommended.

I was saying in blunt terms, concealed by softer presidential language, that the standards of auditing in the profession in the United Kingdom were not good enough and that the Institute had a responsibility to take steps to improve them. I pursued and fostered this policy unceasingly not only in my presidential year but in all the subsequent years I spent on the Council until my retirement from it in 1975. In particular, I advocated the need for auditors to state in the audit report, more often and clearly than they had done in the past, any material matters with which they were dissatisfied and which caused the accounts not to show a true and fair view. An auditing standard on this subject was issued in 1968.

My ambition to improve standards was bound up with the desire to establish a common international attitude. As part of this policy the firm decided to publish that part of our own manual which was concerned with the subject of auditing. It was issued in 1966 as *Cooper's Manual of Auditing*. It has, of course, been revised since and brought up to date and a fourth edition was issued in 1984. It is a standard work on auditing and it is used by students and practitioners in the United Kingdom and overseas.

In the years of growth after the War the firm was at times unpopular. I think it was thought that we were growing too fast which gave rise to some tinges of jealousy among some of our competitors. We were partly to blame for this and were not as sensitive as we should have been to the attitude of colleagues. I was told later that one of the factors which helped to restore the situation was the publication of the manual. The profession realised that we were ready to make available to them in a compact and useful form the benefit of years of work and study, and to share with them a piece of work which had been a not inconsiderable factor in the firm's success in training staff and improving the quality of the firm's work.

Ever since the Institute was formed in 1880 the firm has given unstinting support to its interests. Arthur Cooper was a founder member of the Council and became President in 1883-84 and Ernest Cooper was President from 1899 to 1901. In the last thirty years we have provided five Presidents. Before being elected President, a member of Council will have given many years of work in serving on committees and sub-committees. Apart from that, his partners will also have undertaken a great deal of work serving on the Council or its committees, giving lectures or papers, assisting in training courses and the like. In terms of hours spent, which would otherwise be devoted to earning fees and profits by carrying out professional work for clients, the cost is high but it has always been gladly and willingly given by my firm and by all the other large and medium sized firms. Smaller firms cannot, of course, give as much in total but the proportion of their time which they are willing to give to Institute affairs, including a substantial volume of work in the districts, is no less substantial. This is one of the great strengths of the profession.

The work of the President of the Institute was then, and is now, exhausting. I was asked towards the end of my year to describe how the President passed his time during his year of office. I set out below a brief description I gave then. No doubt the President's duties today are different in form, but I doubt whether they are different in substance.

THE PRESIDENT'S JOB (APRIL 1967)

It takes a long time to become President. It is rare to be elected to the Council much before twenty-five years after qualification and it is normal to serve on the Council for eight to thirteen years before election as President. In my own case, I qualified in 1932, was elected to the Council in 1956 and was appointed President in 1966 at the age of 56. I emphasise this because the younger it is possible to reach the Presidential chair the better. It is a strenuous task and unless the President is mentally and physically fit he cannot do it properly.

The appointment gave me particular satisfaction because I was the third member of the family to hold it; the other two were my great uncles – Arthur Cooper, who held the office in 1883-84, and Ernest Cooper, who was President for two terms (1899-1901).

The President, of course, presides over Council meetings, of which there are at least eleven every year. He cannot do this effectively unless he has a thorough knowledge of Institute affairs, which he acquires in a number of ways.

Unless engaged on other Institute business, the President and the Deputy President attend every meeting of the standing committees of the Council (other than the Investigation and Disciplinary committees). There are fourteen such committees, the majority of which meet monthly; in addition, there are numerous *ad hoc* special committees where the President's attendance is necessary. The task of preparing for these meetings and reading the papers is a heavy one; the weight of paper which has to be gone through each month is measured in pounds, not ounces, and the President must be able to read and absorb quickly. As a result of attending these committee meetings, the President has a remarkable grasp of everything that is passing through the Institute. By his very attendance he can often help to coordinate work which is being done by one committee with work which is going on in another.

During his year of office the President pays a visit to each of the district societies, of which there are sixteen in number. The pattern is usually the same. In the afternoon the President meets the students and has tea with them. At these meetings he addresses them or answers questions about Institute affairs. Later in the evening the President attends the district society dinner and replies to the toast of the Institute, during which he is expected to speak on some topic of professional interest. It is not easy to find sixteen different themes.

The President also presides at a full-day meeting which takes place each year with the Presidents of the district societies, and another meeting with the Union of Chartered Accountants' Students Societies. In addition, the President attends innumerable lunches and dinners given by other professional bodies; he needs a strong head and a sound digestion. He presides over the institute's summer courses held in Oxford and Cambridge each year and attends, or opens, courses and other functions mounted by the Institute. He is required to speak or 'say a few words' and many of these functions.

The labour of making speeches should not be underestimated. If speeches are to have a proper impact it is better that they should be spoken and not read; they should never last more than ten minutes and eight is about the ideal to be aimed at; and they must be full of meat. Any speech which conforms to these standards takes a long time to prepare. In my own case I found that about six hours of work was necessary, often more. Sometimes the President makes visits to meet the Presidents and Councils of professional accountancy bodies overseas. In my own case I travelled about 50,000 miles and spent some six weeks abroad on trips of this nature, during which I made many speeches on the position of the accountancy profession in the United Kingdom.

The task of administering the work of the Institute staff rests on the Secretary, but the President and he are in constant touch, sometimes two and three times a day, discussing Institute affairs, the correspondence which is received from members on a wide variety of matters and, in fact, every topic or event which has, or might have, a bearing on the affairs of the profession. There must be a complete understanding between these two individuals or the Institute affairs will suffer.

These are some of the tasks which the President undertakes in his year of office and there are many more, too numerous to mention. Apart from the above duties the President has another responsibility – to look at the profession and the work of the Institute objectively and as a whole. He must be continually asking himself certain fundamental questions:

- Is the profession going in the right direction?
- What are the long-term objectives?
- What more should it be doing for students and members?
- How does it compare with other professional bodies, particularly those in the accountancy profession?
- Are there any bottlenecks which are holding up progress?

If the President believes that something ought to be done, he has the opportunity and authority to set in hand an enquiry by the appropriate committee to examine the problems so that, if the need be there, action can be taken. It is a thrilling, exciting and exhausting job which absorbs a very high proportion of his working and leisure time. One year is enough.

In 1988 I sat next to a cabinet minister at a dull City dinner. He began by saying that he had always wanted to meet me because he was present when, as President in 1966, I had given an after-dinner address to the Chartered Accountants' Students Society, and that it had made a lasting impression upon him. This sort of flattery gets the stodgiest dinner off to a good start. I did remember making the speech, because at the time I had felt that it was an important occasion and that it might assist students if I said something about their careers in the years to come. I prepared the text carefully and learned it by heart so that I could speak it and not read it. I have since found a copy, which is set out below.

CHARTERED ACCOUNTANTS' STUDENTS SOCIETY (1966)

I learned a salutary lesson about after-dinner speaking when I was in Perth, Australia, not long ago. I was asked to address an audience no less distinguished than this and had prepared myself with care. During dinner my host asked me what I intended to say and I gave him a brief résumé of the best passages. He interrupted me rather rudely and said, 'Man, you can't feed that stuff to this lot; they are only interested in sex and crime.' I see by your eager and expectant faces that you are looking forward to an interesting ten minutes, but the truth of the matter is that I am a bit out of date on one of these subjects and rather shy about my achievements on the other.

At a time when the profession is beginning to spend a good deal of thought on the subject of forecasts, I thought that I might perhaps give you a foretaste of some of the things which I think you will face in the long and exciting years which lie before you.

You will find when you first become qualified and later, when you become a junior partner, that you are not paid enough. You will feel that you are carrying a great burden of work and responsibility and that your seniors, some of them perhaps a little sere and yellow, seem to get disproportionately higher rewards for what they do. You will be quite right about this, but there is nothing that you can do about it. It is a fact of life, to which you must accustom yourselves, that when you are young you are paid less than you are worth and when you are old you tend to be over-rewarded. Do not be despondent – your time will come.

You will also believe that your elders are not adventurous enough. Again, you will be right and again, it is a fact of life. Do not let this frustrate you. Keep your burning enthusiasms; keep thrusting forward and learn to accept with a good grace, occasionally possibly with gratitude, the light reins of restraint with which experience sometimes seeks to curb you.

In the years which follow, every one of you in this hall will be offered bribes and every one of you will accept them. This may shock you, but it is unhappily true. They will not, I hope, be bribes of money. They will be bribes of flattery. It will take many forms, usually something like this. An important client, older than you, will say, 'You seem to me to be a very intelligent young man for your age; you have an old head on young shoulders. Don't you agree with me that . . .' And before you know where you are you will have agreed with a proposition which your professional training and knowledge should have rejected. It takes courage and character to resist these bribes, but if you do so you will enjoy one of the richest prizes open to you – the respect of your fellow men, including your client.

You will find that your clients will make unreasonable demands upon you. They will encroach upon your leisure time; they will expect you and your staff to meet almost impossible deadlines; they will ask for advice at short notice on matters which require many hours of thought and study. This is an occupational disease from which we all suffer but, by a curious paradox, so far from weakening us it keeps us mentally fit and strong.

Your intellectual qualities vary widely. Some of you will seem to succeed with effortless ease. Those of you with lower capacities need not be jealous of your apparently more talented colleagues. Remember the words of Lord Birkenhead: 'How much better it is to be good than brilliant.' You will find that, in the City of London, the men who get to the top are the men who can be trusted. This is the quality above all others which leads to success.

In the course of your life you will unhappily find a few men in the profession who seek to gain temporary popularity or cheap notoriety by denigrating others – the Institute which has sponsored their professional careers; their more successful colleagues; other firms which seem to succeed where theirs has failed. Shun these men. They soon become known and recognised for what they are, and you would be unwise to let yourselves be tarred with the same brush.

There is an agreeable aspect of professional life which I think you will enjoy, and that is the help which you can always obtain for the asking from your professional colleagues, not only in our profession but in the other learned professions. You will find that if ever you are in difficulty or need help, you have but to ask for it and it will be given to you freely and generously. It is one of the characteristics of a profession and, as the years go by, you will get as much pleasure in giving help to your professional brethren as you do from receiving it.

In the course of your careers I think you will find that one of the pleasures of professional practice is your independence. Cherish it at all costs and rejoice in it: your ability to state your opinions fearlessly; your refusal to act for people whom you despise; your ability to concentrate your efforts and serve the public on those aspects of professional practice which most appeal to you. These are all part of the precious right of independence which professional men enjoy.

Finally, you will begin to find very soon in your career that the greatest satisfaction which you achieve is the fact that somebody wants your advice; he needs your skill; he wants you to serve him; he seeks you out because he believes that you, above others, can help him in his problems and his difficulties. When this happens you will be justly proud and pleased, and the thrill lasts as long as you continue to practise. It will spur you to greater efforts. One thing only may sometimes mar your satisfaction. You will often be humbled by your own inadequacy.

I hope you will not think that these are all fanciful promises. It is because they have happened in the past that I think they may happen to you in the future. I shall feel rewarded if some of you recognise them in the years to come.

It is usual to conclude addresses of this nature in a frivolous vein. I am in no mood to do so. I would like you to remember that we have the privilege of belonging to a private organisation which serves the public interest. In fulfilling your share of these obligations, you will often be faced with doubts and anxieties. In such circumstances strength and courage are sometimes to be found in a simple belief or creed. It is for each of you to choose his own. It is, therefore, with some diffidence that I offer four short lines which seem to me to epitomise everything that is important to a member of this Institute:

> I would be true, for there are those who trust me;
> I would be pure, for there are those who care;
> I would be strong, for there is much to suffer;
> I would be brave, for there is much to dare.

When I was elected to the Council in 1956 the constitution provided that Council members were elected by the Council itself. In later years this arrangement was thought to be undemocratic and appointments to the Council are now by election of the members in the area in which the member carries on business. It is less satisfactory. If a profession is to be strong and vigorous, the members of the governing body should be of the highest possible quality and attainments and, on the whole, the original system achieved this because members were elected on the basis of their known achievements and quality. The present system does not always do so. The members cast their votes based on a very short description of the candidate on the agenda paper and they cannot know the relevant competence and ability of those who are up for election. It therefore becomes somewhat of a lottery and there have been many cases where men of great ability have not been elected and members of lesser attainments have been chosen in their place.

I am no longer in the corridors of power and propose no solution, but merely point out the defects of the present situation. It can be overcome in part because the Council has the right to appoint a proportion of 'co-opted' members and good men are put on the Council by this means. I was one of those who was careful to insist on this provision at the time the constitution was changed, but it is not the best remedy.

Despite the progress we had made in expanding the firm

overseas, especially in the British Commonwealth, we were weak in America. In 1956 an incident occurred which had profound effects. I was at a conference with counsel, Charles Russell QC (later Lord Russell of Killowen), in the middle of which I was asked to take a telephone call in the clerk's room, which is not a convenient place for a business discussion. An American voice said over the telephone that he was speaking from New York. He asked whether I would like to take on $40,000 worth of work. I was a bit nonplussed and said, 'Yes please.' It emerged that it was the senior partner of Lybrand, Ross Bros and Montgomery, a large and successful American firm who had shortly before made contact with the partner in charge of our small office in New York. He came to London and asked us to take on the work of Lybrand's offices in London and Paris. John Pears and I were delighted by this approach. We asked them to consider a full merger of our respective interests in all parts of the world and then to practice worldwide under a common international name. They were not at that time willing to consider this; they wanted to be rid of two overseas offices which were proving difficult to manage and which gave them problems of administration. Nevertheless, John and I felt that this was the start of the organisation we wanted to achieve. John and I later went to New York to finalise the arrangement; we found on arrival that there had been a change of heart and that our new friends were prepared to consider a much wider association.

We got down to negotiating the organisation which John and I had wanted from the beginning. We reached agreement fairly quickly and a new and substantial international firm was brought into being on 1 January 1957. There was a good deal of discussion about the name. Should Lybrand come first or Coopers? After much bargaining the name of Coopers & Lybrand was settled for all Lybrand's overseas work but the name of Lybrand, Ross Bros & Montgomery was retained in America. A few years later, in 1973, the final step was taken and we practised worldwide as Coopers & Lybrand. The merger which began in 1957 gave rise to a great deal of additional professional work for the firm in all parts of the world.

Over thirty years ago I was asked by the young men who were then being admitted as junior partners to set down some of my experiences in moving from a junior to a senior partner and to give them guidance on how they could make the best contribution to the firm. In particular they wanted to know how a partner managed to get new work. I hesitated about publishing this because now it seems to me to be routine stuff. However, the simple principles laid down were part of the foundations on which the firm was built and they are not always appreciated. They may possibly be of some interest to chartered accountants who are about to be admitted to partnership. I have therefore reproduced the advice I gave to them as an appendix to this chapter and I have no wish to change it now (see pages 66-79).

Some time later I was asked to set down the duties and responsibilities of the senior partner of the firm. I do not think it would be of interest to set these out in full, but there was one paragraph which indicated the mental and physical stress which anyone holding that position has to undergo. It read as follows:

It is a hard job, physically and mentally, and needs abounding energy. It is impossible to do it unless the senior partner keeps himself fit. I spend, on average, two to three nights every week in the year out late or away from home altogether. On the nights when I am at home I usually have to spend some time reading papers. The constant unceasing interruptions caused by the duties described above mean that thinking work, drafting work, and professional work require at least half a day and sometimes a full working day every weekend. I daresay my successor will be able to organise himself better.

The measure of the firm's growth in the post-war period can best be expressed in figures. The following table indicates the growth at intervals of five years from 1945 until I retired in 1975.

Growth in numbers

	UK firm	International firm (this figure includes those in column 1)	Offices worldwide
1945	173	239	8
1950	352	991	35
1955	396	1,294	53
1960	653	4,172	76
1965	1,070	7,831	123
1970	1,897	13,627	172
1975	2,207	18,386	332

The worldwide strength of the firm at the time of writing (1989) is over 45,000.

While I was with Coopers it was my life, and practically everything else was subordinated to it. The dedication was, for practical purposes, complete. I do not think it was a personal ambition but there was a definite wish to see the *firm* recognised as one of the best and as a leader in the profession. At one of the annual dinners which we gave to the staff (later abandoned because no London hotel could cope with the numbers) I said that if anyone was going to succeed in the profession he must be dedicated to it. It seemed a harmless comment at the time but the following day five or six of the staff tendered their resignations. They felt, I suppose, that they could not commit themselves to a doctrine of dedication and, without it, they felt that their future in the firm was bleak.

In the post-war years the firm developed a reputation for large-scale investigations. The scope for this type of work was, and is still, considerable and it arises in many ways. The developed countries make large sums available for foreign aid or investment abroad. They need the services of accountants to examine these projects in the planning stages and possibly to watch their progress while they are being executed. Other countries are in a process of developing and their governments are anxious to have advice on new projects about to be undertaken. An industry may be passing through a lean period and an appraisal of its present difficulties and its future prospects may be required. A large industrial concern may wish to start a new enterprise in the home market or to establish a subsidiary abroad, and be anxious to check its assessment of the capital expenditure involved and the prospects of the venture proving profitable. A government or a large organisation may be troubled by a particular problem in the financial or industrial field which requires independent enquiry.

Most decisions are relatively easy if all the facts of a situation are properly marshalled in their proper order and with a sense of proportion. Fact finding is one of the main functions which an accountant is fitted to perform and it is one of the reasons why he is so often called upon to undertake these special studies. There is no easy way of finding all the facts. It involves a carefully prepared plan of campaign followed by days or weeks of hard slogging; examination and cross examination; the sifting of masses of figures and paper to select the things which really matter. It requires a specialised staff who can devote their whole time to the job and are not distracted by being asked to deal with a number of other assignments at the same time. The preparation of the report stresses the need for an accountant to be able to express himself clearly and succinctly in the English tongue. It is one thing to write a report which is addressed to a client who may be indulgent about occasional short lapses; it is quite another to write a report which may be the subject of a debate in Parliament where every word may be subject to criticism and upon which the reputation of the firm depends.

Assignments of this character carry a good deal of prestige and are widely commented upon in the professional and, sometimes, the national press. This raises the reputation of the firm which carries them out and the standing of the accountancy profession as a whole is enhanced. The public become accustomed to turn to members of the profession when national problems arise which require dispassionate enquiry and a balanced conclusion. Very often the work, when it is done, is a means of saving many millions of pounds or of creating work for, or saving the jobs of, many hundreds of employees. There is no work which is more satisfying for an accountant or one which fulfils so well the purpose of the profession.

I got job satisfaction from a problem or a situation which needed careful anaylsis from which conclusions could be drawn or recommendations put forward. I also took pleasure in presenting the analysis and conclusions in simple language. Apart, therefore, from the day-to-day work of an accountant's office I was often asked to chair or sit as a member of a committee which was charged with the task of making an enquiry of one sort or another. These investigations can be very time-consuming. If one is chairman it is relatively easy to arrange a programme to suit one's own convenience and keep the discussion on the rails; otherwise meetings are often called on inconvenient dates and time has to be spent listening to the views of other members of the committee which are sometimes clear and coherent but sometimes prolix and confused.

The early chapters have given an account of my early life and the War years, and the background to my professional life as a partner in Coopers. I have put in an appendix at the end of this book (see pages 229-234) a list of some of the public and semi-public assignments I undertook and the remaining chapters describe a few of them and any unusual features about them which seem worth recording.

None of this work could, of course, have been undertaken without the back-up of my firm. I was able, to whatever extent was necessary, to draw on the advice and help of partners and staff at all levels to provide support. In reading any of the accounts which follow I hope this invaluable background service will be borne in mind, because without it I could have achieved very little.

During those busy years, I wrote countless articles and made scores of speeches on every aspect of business life and the work of an accountant. On glancing through those where I have retained copies, I notice that they reflect the conditions prevailing at the time, and many of them are now out of date. The remainder have material in them which is still relevant today, despite the march of time. Occasionally I have used them to help in compiling these pages, but I think they would be boring, except for somebody who wished to wallow in professional history, so I have left them undisturbed to gather dust.

APPENDIX

NOTES FOR A JUNIOR PARTNER ON JOINING THE FIRM (MAY 1957)

1.   The idea of writing this paper did not germinate in my mind. It was suggested to me that it would be worthwhile putting on paper my own experiences in graduating from a junior partner into a senior partner, so that the junior partners of the future might know some of the problems of this metamorphosis. It is not suggested that all partners should conform to a common mould, as one of the benefits of partnership is to get the different views and opinions of a number of people who approach problems in different ways. This paper is concerned, therefore, with some suggestions which may help junior partners to carry out their work quickly and efficiently, and not with the decisions which they ultimately arrive at on any particular subject. Much of what I write will sound priggish or pompous – so be it. It is an inevitable consequence of trying to put this sort of thing into writing.

Disillusionment
2.   After the thrill of having a room to yourself and signing the firm's name for the first time, you usually find that life is not at all what you expected it to be. You still seem to have to do much the same sort of work you had to do as a manager instead of having, as you believed, rows of willing

managers to do it for you. You have to work much harder than when you were on the staff and at a much higher pitch of concentration. You are constantly summoned to your senior partner's presence to clear up some untidy little mess or extra task which he does not want to do himself, and when you finally do complete your first few jobs and take them to a senior partner for a little congratulation and encouragement, you probably find that most of your work is roughly handled and is sent back to be done again.

3.   There is a great deal of truth in all this and one reason for it is that we have always believed in making partners when they were young – many years younger than in most firms. As a result the junior partner gets a slightly inflated sense of his significance before he has earned his position in the firm. The senior partners, on the other hand, forget how inexperienced the latest member of the firm really is and expect him (quite unreasonably) to have qualities and an experience which they themselves have taken years to achieve.

Organising yourself

4.   The first thing a junior partner has to learn to do is to organise himself. As a member of the staff you have usually been able to concentrate on one or two jobs only, but as soon as you become a partner you find that you have to watch a great many and to put up with innumerable interruptions besides. The only way to do this is to list all your work and to mark it off in order of priority so that you know exactly what you have got to accomplish and the date by which it has to be done. The mere listing of it is an admirable way of clearing your mind about what has to be done and by what date. It brings home to you how much more you can achieve by careful planning and by not wasting time on unimportant matters.

Delegation

5.   The next thing is to decide what you can do yourself and what you cannot or ought not to do. The whole of the latter

category has to be delegated and the sooner you learn how to delegate the better. The art of delegation is easy to acquire once you have made up your mind that you are going to do it. Send for your secretary and dictate a note to whomsoever you are going to delegate the job. Dictate precisely (a) what has to be done and (b) the date by which it has to be completed. Not only will you have cleared your own mind as to the task, but you will have observed the fundamental principle of delegation, namely that the person to whom you have delegated knows precisely what he has to do. Tell your secretary to keep a copy of the note and to let you have it some time before the due date. This gives you time to put pressure on the delegatee for prompt delivery and enables you to organise your own diary to deal with it in most cases; mere delegation won't, of course, finish the job. You will have to have discussions with the delegatee from time to time and review his work, in the course of which you may have to revise your instructions.

Your secretary

8.   The next thing to do is to learn how to dictate. Before you do this get a competent secretary. It is no use complaining that your secretary is hopeless, or cannot take down dictation fast enough, or has no common sense. The solution is in your hands entirely and a partner gets no better secretary than he deserves. Don't put up with incompetent secretaries and go on choosing your own until you get efficiency. I am satisfied that a partner's personal output can be increased by 50 per cent merely by having a good secretary.

Learning to dictate

7.   Never put pen to paper if you can possibly avoid it. Make yourself dictate until you dictate better than you write. With very difficult drafts or writing the conclusions to a report, audit qualfications and the like, you often have to write longhand, but let these be the exceptions rather than the rule. But there is a method in dictation like everything

else. Don't just send for your secretary and give a garbled draft. List on a slip of paper all the points you want to make and then mark them (1), (2), (3) – and so on in the order in which they should be dictated – then dictate from that. It means that you will have channelled your thoughts properly before you begin and your dictation will begin to flow freely.

Making up your own mind

8.   The next thing to do is to learn to make up your own mind first. I believe it is the most important piece of self-discipline which a partner has to teach himself. There is a natural instinct in all of us to refrain from making a decision if somebody else will do it for us. This is particularly the case where you have partners and particularly (as you believe) senior partners who seem to like making decisions and who always seem to want their own way. In fact, you do your senior partners less than justice.

9.   What happens in practice is that a junior partner meets a problem. He knows it is a difficult one and he therefore gathers up his papers and goes to see another partner and may have the good or ill fortune to find a senior partner who has some time to spare. The senior partner has probably seen this type of problem before and drawing on his past experience asks half a dozen crucial questions to which the junior partner does not know the answers. This is bound to lead to trouble. With, as he thinks, the best intentions the junior partner has gone to a senior partner to ask for advice and much to his chagrin all he gets is a request to go and find out a great deal more information or to do the job properly. The fault, in fact, is the junior partner's. He should know *not some, but all, the facts thoroughly* and before he leaves his room he should have *made up his own mind quite clearly and definitely* what the correct answer should be and the reasons why he has come to that conclusion. If it is a question of writing a letter, he should have written the letter in draft in a form in which he is satisfied it can be sent out without modification. The original decision may prove to be wrong or to need modification but that should not prevent

the junior partner always making up his mind first. It is also the quickest possible way to gain experience. If your original decision is confirmed you will have gone through all the thought processes necessary to arrive at the right conclusion and will never have to do it again for the rest of your professional life. If you have arrived at the wrong decision, the exposure of your incorrect thought processes will be equally valuable experience.

10.   Another manifestation of this failure to make up one's mind occurs when a senior partner asks a junior partner to do a job. The senior partner knows perfectly well there are perhaps six easy points and two difficult ones. A day or two later, possibly a week or more, the junior partner appears with the draft letter answering all the easy points but leaving blanks for the difficult ones saying, 'I don't know what you want to say at this point.' The senior partner quells a feeling of inward rage and settles down to do the job himself. It would have been much quicker if he had done it himself in the first place. What the senior partners want is not somebody who comes back without the answer but a junior partner who comes back with what he believes to be the best answer, clearly expressed. A junior partner who organises himself on that basis is what a senior partner prays for.

11.   This emphasis on making up your mind should never, however, stop discussion. The immense advantage of partnership is that you can talk things over with different types of people who have different ideas. This will stimulate your thoughts and your partners' also. *Many partners do not seem to realise this and keep themselves and their jobs to themselves far too much.* All I am trying to say in the three preceding paragraphs is that you mustn't allow other people to do your thinking for you, so that when you discuss things, you know not only the facts but also have positive ideas and a contribution to make.

What gets and keeps clients

12.   Ever since I first became a parent, I wondered what advice I should give to a child if he or she wanted to know

what would cause him or her to be a success in life. It matters not that no child of mine has ever thought of asking and, on present form, would flatly disagree even if the advice were tendered. The fact remains that I think there are four qualities and they are the same qualities which beget and keep clients. In order of importance they are first trustworthiness, second energy, third a sense of proportion or common sense, and fourth cleanliness. The second and fourth lie in your own hands; the first and third are partly instinctive and the less instinctive they are the harder you have to work to reach an unattainable goal. I don't propose to dilate any further on this choice, else this paper would read like a sermon. You can take them or leave them as you like. The only thing which is worth commenting on is perhaps this. A group of leaders of industry were asked to give the one quality which, above everything else contributed, in their opinion, to their success. By a huge margin the answer was energy. Nevertheless I put it second, certainly in professional life.

13. If you are ever going to be any good as a professional accountant you must know your client and his business thoroughly. You ought to be on Christian-name terms with all clients of about your own age, and most of your clients who are older than you should call you by your Christian name. A client does not usually want to talk to you about routine audit points. He wants to discuss his results, his staff, his plans, his future and provision for his wife and family. In particular, he wants to know how he can improve his business or his own affairs, as the case may be, and to be kept informed on the latest ideas in finance and accounting. That means you have got to think about him and his business quite apart from the points which are brought up on the audit. In short, you have always got to put yourself into his shoes. It is no use marking off the audit papers and, with a sigh of relief, striking another job off your list. What have you done constructively to help the client? What changes in his business would you make if you were in the client's shoes? It is the partner who thinks on these lines

who makes the difference between the business getter and the pedestrian accountant.

14.   Another example of the same point occurs in your own approach to the client. When I was an articled clerk one of our clients had a legal problem. We went to see the company's solicitor who said what the client wanted to do was impossible. Not content, the client took me round to get another opinion from another solicitor, who was one of the leading solicitors in London. The second repeated exactly what the first had said but in the same breath said, 'Let's see how we can meet the problem' and immediately began exploring half a dozen different ideas out of which a good plan emerged. It sounds so obvious and elementary as scarcely to be worth recording but it impressed me (and the client) a great deal at the time. No partner should ever turn down a client's proposal without immediately trying to suggest an alternative. It is sometimes impossible but at least the client thinks you have tried, which is what matters.

15.   Another variation of the theme is not to take 'no' for an answer. It is surprising how often one can achieve what at first sight appears impossible by the simple process of deciding that the common sense of a problem indicates a certain solution and sticking at it until this result is achieved. You may be dealing with an intransigent inspector or estate duty officer; you may want a client to change his fixed opinions; you may want to secure a certain piece of work or to establish a certain contact; you may want an increased fee. These, and other difficulties like them, can usually be surmounted by sticking at it. It requires a sense of proportion to know when the task is really impossible – and that cannot be acquired except by experience; but the first thing that is necessary is the determination not to be defeated.

16.   When you go to see a client, organise your mind and the interview in advance. Separate the important matters from the unimportant and make up your mind on the point you want to establish in each case. Also ask yourself what the client's reaction is likely to be and what you would say if

you were in his shoes. This will enable you to be forearmed against possible resistance to your points. Start the interview by saying, 'I have got three points of principle and half a dozen minor points to deal with at the end.' Nothing makes an auditor look more foolish than to discuss, say, a real point of principle on, say, stock valuation followed by a discussion on missing petty cash vouchers.

17.   Moreover, when you go round on audit to discuss points on the client's accounts, make up your mind before you go (a) what you are going to stand firm on and (b) what you will try and get him to accept but won't (for adequate reasons) stand firm on. An auditor loses his client's respect altogether if he makes a great song and dance about a point and finally, under pressure from the client, gives way. And it is wise to have a word with another partner before you make up your mind what you will stand firm on, so that if it really comes to an issue your partners will not torpedo you.

18.   Another quality which attracts work is a mastery of the English tongue. Clear letters and reports in non-technical language which are understood at the first reading mean much more to the clients than long paragraphs of technical jargon, however perfect they may be from an academic point of view. At board meetings a few short sentences clearly enunciated and expressed are worth infinitely more than a long discourse, however erudite.

A sense of urgency

19.   One faculty which all junior partners seem to lack is a sense of urgency. It takes a noticeable time for this trait to develop. If you go to a doctor you do not want to wait ten days for a diagnosis and if you go to your tailor you do not want to wait a month for a fitting. Clients want their work done promptly and by a stated time and, if a professional office is to keep lively and vigorous, work must be cleared up quickly. Anything from 10 to 25 per cent of my time is spent in chasing junior partners to see that work is done. It is a most exhausting process, both for the chased and the chaser, and ought not to be necessary to anything like the

extent that in fact it proves to be. The cause is partly due to the fact that junior partners have not lived through the era in the firm's history when it was stagnant. They do not know the abounding energy and thrust which was necessary to overcome this complacency; to remake the firm's reputation; to get the flow of work coming back into the firm; to build and expand at home and abroad. Now they see the work flowing in and swamping them it is difficult for them to realise that the flow will soon stop unless the work is cleared quickly so that partners are eager and always looking out for more.

Staff

20.   The secret of getting the best from the staff is knowing how far you can trust each member of the staff with the work which he is given to do. With the tried hands, it is not difficult because the senior partners will have assessed the work of each of them over many years and can indicate just how far you can go. The difficulty arises with the newer staff who the senior partners have not seen so much of and who the junior partners have to assess for themselves. There is no quick road to success; it is a long process of testing until you have seen the member of the staff in a sufficient number of different situations and different jobs to enable you to decide how reliable his work and his judgement are. It is also most important because junior partners must learn to spot the managers of the future. Curiously enough, it will often be found that a manager's judgement is sound but the reliability of his figures and arithmetic uncertain. The reverse is also true.

21.   One thing junior partners must make up their minds about from the first day as a partner is that they will not accept shoddy work. It requires a lot of courage when a manager of long years of standing brings a poor letter, a bad report, an ill-laid out schedule or a half-completed audit, to reject it and require it to be done again – but it has got to be done with what tact you can muster. Once the staff realise that you will not accept shoddy work that class of work will

not be presented to you and everyone is happier as a consequence.

22.   One other point to remember is that managers want help. When I was an articled clerk I spent many interesting hours with the managers discussing the quality of the partners. I expected them to say that the then senior partner was impossible to work for, as at times he was known to be rough and unreasonable. The verdict was quite different. The senior partner came off with high marks. The reasons were quite simply stated:

1. 'Once he gets on to a job he clears his work quickly, with common sense and without fuss.'
2. 'If you go and tell him you are in trouble, either with too much work or with a problem which is bothering you, he will take endless pains to help you out of it.'

Those two qualities outstripped all the other adverse factors. Other partners at that time, who always seemed outwardly pleasant to deal with, or more easy-going and less exacting, were not so well thought of because they dithered or procrastinated, or would not make up their minds, or took a long and tortuous way round instead of the direct and short route to the point, or choked over the gnats and swallowed the whales.

23.   Staff will not stand sarcasm. They do not mind your being outspoken provided you are fair; they do not mind your being exacting provided it is done without fuss. They have every bit as much pride in the firm as you have and enjoy watching the firm doing well and, like all of us, they realise that only happens if the highest quality of work is produced.

Getting to know people

24.   The junior partners often wonder how senior partners get work. Work comes from reputation and by being known by and to a large number of people. Reputation is built

largely on the quality and characteristics which have been mentioned earlier in this paper. There is also the problem of getting known, as the spread of reputation simply by word of mouth from one person to another is comparatively slow. It follows that junior partners have got to get to know people and to impress their personality upon them. This requires effort. It means seeking people out, or asking them to lunch and being asked to lunch and other functions. Any partner who lunches alone more than one or at most two days a week is not doing his job; he ought to be out lunching with somebody. If he sees from his diary that he has blank lunch days ahead of him, he should make a list of all the people he wants to get to know and ring them up until he has filled his diary. Do not be frightened of being snubbed because it seldom happens; and it is also worth remembering that a lot of people are anxious to get to know junior partners in the firm. It is also worth remarking that one never meets someone without picking up some useful piece of information or hearing a different viewpoint from one's own. These meetings, therefore, all help to provide one with experience of one sort or another.

25.   When meeting a client at lunch, it is no use merely arranging for the food to be served properly. You want to make up your mind beforehand what you can *give* the client by way of suggestions or what thoughts you can put into his mind on which you can speak with authority. There is always something new – pension schemes, some new tax point, estate duty. A client should always leave you feeling he has gained something from the meeting; when a difficulty next comes up he will think of you and that breeds work. The reason why a professional man's life is so exhausting is because he is 'giving out' the whole day long from 9 till 6 and often in the evenings besides.

26.   You will find, as the years go by, that the two really exciting things in professional life are first, the thrill of the chase, that is to say, getting a new job; second, the feeling that somebody wants to have your particular advice because he thinks that you can help him better than anybody else.

These two exciting things can be achieved only by getting to know, and getting to be known by, people.

Recreation

27.   Another essential thing is for you to have at least one other occupation, hobby or sport which you do reasonably well. It does not much matter what it is – golf, tennis, shooting, sailing, fishing, painting, stamp collecting, or anything else – but it must be something at least which gives your professional life a better balance and makes you more interesting to clients. A partner who can only talk with authority about balance sheets is indeed a dull dog and is unlikely to breed new clients or hold old ones.

Administration

28. Junior partners do not realise for some time the immense amount of administration which is required to make the firm work smoothly both at home and in its overseas relationships. It has taken years of work and patience to get it to its present pitch and by comparison with other firms I think it stands well in that respect; but the administration can slip very quickly if it is not constantly watched.

29.   It has been the practice in the past to apportion the supervisory administrative work among various partners, but there has been a noticeable tendency, after two or three years, for partners to say they are tired of it, or would like a rest from it, or would like some other partner to take it on. This is a wholly unrealistic attitude. The administration has to be spread among all the partners and constant change in the supervising partner does not do any good at all. Moreover, unless junior partners become thoroughly familiar with the administrative work of the firm, they will never be any good as senior partners later on. In short, you have got to find out how the firm works in all its aspects from the moment the letters are delivered in the morning to the time when the last member cf staff leaves at night, and if

you are given a slice of this work to supervise, you have got to be on top of the job the whole time.

The senior partner as a chameleon

30.   It has sometimes astonished junior partners to see how forceful and forthright senior partners can be with the staff and partners of the firm in the office and how suave and conciliatory they can be with directors and staff of client firms. Junior partners tend to feel that this is unreasonable and that if clients, some of whom are obviously inefficient, can be treated tenderly there is no reason why they should not be treated in the same way. This is due to confusion of two different things. Cooper Brothers & Co is a very large administrative machine. It requires a very great effort to keep it moving efficiently at the right pace and in the right direction and anybody or anything which stops or checks that effort has to be pushed along, albeit sometimes a little roughly. Clients are in a quite different position. *They are there to be served* and they are paying for the service and they know both those things very well. They expect their sensibilities to be pandered to and, if they are not, will seek some other adviser.

Professional etiquette

31.   You must know the normal rules of professional etiquette because some members of the profession spend time looking for complaints to lay before the investigation committee of the Institute, and the partners of the larger firms are particularly vulnerable. A fairly good summary of the position is set out in an article I wrote in 1956, which you should read, together with the reading matter referred to in that article.

Getting people to agree with you

32.   Finally, there is one last piece of experience which is worth noting down. If you know the facts of the situation clearly there is seldom much difficulty in deciding what to do. The great difficulty is persuading other people of the

necessity to do it. When planning any project, it is no use setting aside 90 per cent of your efforts in deciding on the right course and 10 per cent on getting it done. You have got to plan your work differently to set aside about 50 per cent of your efforts in deciding what to do and 50 per cent in getting everybody else to agree to it, even apparently the most obvious things.

Conclusion

33. I apologise for this harangue. You probably do not agree with it or feel that 'things don't work out that way for you'. All I can say is that they worked out that way for me.

ADDENDUM

The percentages in the penultimate paragraph are, on reflection, incorrect. As I have mentioned earlier a few percentage points have to be spent in deciding what to do and the remaining 90 odd percentage points in persuading other people.

4.

The Conduct of
Large-Scale Investigations

I have often been asked to set out in detail how one begins,
and later carries out, a major investigation of the type
described in the preceding chapter. Every one is different,
depending on its purpose, but the basic technique is much
the same in all cases. It is prudent to study the terms of
reference carefully in order to understand what is required.
Very often these are casually or imprecisely drawn and, if
so, it is essential to get them clearly specified so that there
will not be disappointment when the report is published.

Investigations of this character make it necessary to be
able to draw upon a wide general knowledge of men and
affairs, social and economic conditions, political thought
and, when the occasion demands it, the special conditions
which operate in overseas territories. For example, it is
futile to attempt an assessment of the capital costs of a large
project in the middle of Africa without a very clear
knowledge of the economic, labour, transport and living
conditions there and the probable effect of inflation on the
cost of goods which are not due for delivery for some years
and are being supplied by many different countries. These
special investigations need, above everything else, common
sense. Very often the highly skilled technician arrives at the
wrong practical answer; conversely, the man of limited
technical knowledge but with a wide administrative
experience knows instinctively what the sensible solution
is. Common sense is in any case an essential ingredient in
the make-up of a good accountant and, insofar as it is not
inherent, it is forced upon him by clients.

The first task is to break the subject down into a number of
separate subheadings or topics. The initial topics are usually

easy to discern, but as the investigation proceeds it may be necessary to add others. Merely by way of example, if the investigator is required to place a value on a business which is a going concern, the obvious major topics for consideration are the turnover and profits; the value of the assets; the management; and the future prospects. As the enquiry develops, other topics may need to be added, such as the current or foreseeable competition; the opportunities for expansion at home and abroad; the need to expand some lines of production or to curtail others; the existence of an unsound liquid position; or the carrying of excessive stock-in-trade.

One advantage of proceeding in this way is that it makes it easy to organise the work of the investigating team. A large job may involve as many as twenty or thirty staff. If junior partners or senior members of the staff are each given a topic (or a series of topics) to deal with, the work can be delegated to them in an orderly way. Each of the staff to whom work is delegated should be told at the outset, preferably in writing, what he is expected to do and, when possible, the date by which he is expected, with the help of subordinate staff, to complete the task.

The next task is to make a list of the information which is needed under each topic, so as to be sure that all the essential facts are available on which an opinion can be expressed. This is where the skill of the investigator and his staff begins to show itself. As I have already pointed out, if all the facts of a situation are carefully marshalled, without bias and in a logical order (which is one of the main objectives of every investigation), the answers usually stand out for themselves. The task, therefore, is to decide what information is needed before a balanced decision can be made. It requires many hours of thought, not only to decide what is needed, but how and from whom it can best be obtained in the shortest possible time. Some of the topics involve detailed studies or research projects to seek out information or figures which are not readily available because their importance has not previously been recognised. These studies often take a considerable time and expose facets of the problem which are of great significance. They must, therefore, be set in hand early in the investigation.

In Chapter 10 I criticise the quality of the Green Papers, issued in February 1989, setting out the Government's proposals for the future work and organisation of the legal profession. Questions were put to the Lord Chancellor in the House of Lords in May 1989 asking what research studies had been undertaken and whether they could be examined by the public. It emerged that no research studies had been set in hand before the Green Papers were laid before Parliament. This failure to undertake enquiries which are invariably made in an enterprise of this character partially explains the poor quality of the Green Papers and the criticisms which ensued when they were issued.

One helpful way of getting the essential facts is to prepare a series of questions to which the enquirer wants an answer. On one large enquiry I undertook, I went on a Mediterranean cruise just after the enquiry began. There is nothing much to do on a cruise, so I spent time, and got a good deal of pleasure, in putting down every question I could think of; some were simple and routine, some were awkward and penetrating. In the end I amassed a total of about 1,500 questions. When I returned to London these were sorted under some forty different topics and the skeleton of the enquiry had thus taken shape.

If the investigation is a private enquiry which does not involve members of the public, it is necessary to make a list of all the people in the organisation whom it is necessary to see, and the order in which this should take place. Every interview needs preparation beforehand. A list must be prepared of the points or questions to which an answer is required, but it must be realised, of course that numerous other points will arise in the course of the discussion. Very often charts, schedules or summaries have to be prepared in advance so that the contents, or the conclusions to be drawn from them, can be teased out during the oral discussion. A single interview with a witness is often not enough, because there is so much ground to be covered. In addition, where the views of the witnesses are contradictory, the differences have to be exposed and examined on their merits with the persons concerned.

Witnesses vary enormously. Some are wary that the final report may criticise them and are, therefore, sensitive and on the defensive, and inclined to be reticent. Some are anxious to talk – often because they want to put the blame on other shoulders. Some welcome the enquiry, in the hope that it will resolve problems which have been plaguing them for a long while. Usually there are one or two people in the second line of management who are not worried about their personal positions, but have been watching a developing situation for a long while without the power or opportunity to do anything about it. They talk freely and without bias, and their evidence is usually of great value.

Unless a tape recording is made at the time it is necessary always to have at least one junior partner or skilled member of the staff sitting in on these interviews, with whom the investigator can discuss the result of the interview and so that a careful note can be made of what transpired. These notes should be expanded into a fuller record immediately afterwards. Each such record should be initialled and dated by the investigator-in-chief and his assistant, in case there is any dispute at a later date about what took place.

All this work is exhausting and time-consuming, but if it is done properly it is not long before the main problems and difficulties are isolated. The investigator can then concentrate his enquiries on these matters, until he is satisfied in his own mind that he has established the essential facts and is able to come to a reasonable conclusion.

If the enquiry is not private and involves a matter of public interest it is usual to advertise it and invite members of the public to make submissions. It is also necessary to write to every person or organisation who could be expected to make a contribution, and to ask him or it to give evidence. It is desirable to ask for views in writing, so that if oral evidence is given later, either voluntarily or at the investigator's request, there is some specific material on which the oral dialogue can be based. When writing to possible witnesses, it is helpful to ask each witness to give his views on certain specific matters which are stated in the letter. In many cases the letter should be expanded to include a list of questions, under each topic, which witnesses are asked to answer. The several replies which come in help to establish the facts, and indicate whether the point is one on which there is dispute or whether it is a controversial matter which will need further probing. A comparison of answers to the same question from many responsible witnesses is invaluable in getting to the heart of any problem.

The volume of written material which comes in from witnesses in a public company is usually formidable. The solution is to make a copy of each witness's evidence and cut it up so that the evidence relevant to each separate topic can be filed under that topic. When the text of the report is being written all the evidence which has been tendered is thus already assembled under each topic. Good filing staff are essential, because if the work of filing the evidence gets into arrears, it requires superhuman efforts to get it up to date. Moreover in a public enquiry when several hundred submissions may be recorded, it is usual for any person who wishes to do so to be allowed to read the evidence. This means that, from the outset a careful record of each piece of evidence has to be kept, together with an up-to-date list of witnesses in alphabetical order.

It is my practice to read all the answers which come in from witnesses. If I notice a point of importance, I dictate a short note, and I also do this after each witness has given oral evidence. If I remember that an earlier witness has expressed a different view, I record that in the note as well. These notes are filed under topics. When engaged on a big investigation it is never out of one's mind so that odd points occur to one at different times of the day and often in a waking hour in the middle of the night. I dictate a note of these points as soon as possible which is filed with the notes I have described, in topic order. When arrangements are made to start drafting the report, this accumulation of important points on each topic, coupled with the files of relevant evidence referred to above, provides invaluable material on which the text of the report can be based.

The writing of the report is a heavy task. The final conclusions and opinions cannot be arrived at until the end of the enquiry, but it is a mistake to leave the whole task to the end. A great deal of background material, factual information, and statistics where relevant, can be put together under each topic while it is fresh in mind, and the text can be added to from time to time, in these respects, as the enquiry proceeds. It would, in my view, be impracticable to leave the whole of the report writing process until the enquiry had been completed, because of the time it takes to do so and because the emphasis which needs to be given to certain points may be overlooked. For example, the report of the Royal Commission on Legal Services comprised forty-four chapters and over 1,600 pages of printed text. It would have taken a year to write the report if we had waited until all the evidence had been received, and by that time the relative importance of some of the evidence received would have faded.

Some people believe that an investigator should not make up his mind about any of the issues involved until the end of the enquiry. I have not found this either sensible or practicable. I usually make up my mind quite early and provisionally on what I think the main answers or recommendations should be, but well realising that these opinions may be wrong. The advantage of this process is that one tests all the evidence as it comes in, against a provisional view, which means that the evidence is subjected to a critical assessment as soon as it is received. Moreover, the investigator can put specific questions to witnesses to test the soundness or otherwise of his provisional views. This process goes on throughout the whole period of the enquiry, with the result that each point is sifted, tested and analysed, so that at the end of the day the investigator has a pretty sure idea of the answers or recommendations he proposes to make. I have noticed with interest that in virtually every investigation I have carried out I have started out in the belief that the correct answers lie in one direction, only to find, as the text of the report is put down on paper, that it leads in a greater or lesser degree to different answers.

I prefer that the first draft of the report should be written by a junior partner or member of the staff and this is, of course, necessary in a large enquiry where various topics are delegated. Thereafter it is a time-consuming and exhausting task to go through it line by line until one is satisfied with the result. Very few reports which I have put my name to have taken less than five or six drafts. The process works like this:

1. First preliminary draft put together by a junior partner or a member (or members) of staff.
2. The second draft which includes the major changes which are inevitably necessary to the first crude draft under 1.
3. The third draft should put the report into a quarter-final state, but there will still be a number of inconsistencies, gaps in the information, errors, mistakes of grammar, wrong use of tenses and other lacunae.
4. The fourth draft is, one hopes, the semi-final and, if the polishing and pruning go well, it leads to be completed report.

There are often one or more additional drafts between stages three and four. In practice, moreover, some sections or chapters always prove difficult and they are revised or altered not once, but sometimes over and over again. The typing and rapid production of drafts is a considerable task and the benefit of having word processors and highly skilled typists who use common sense and are consistent in the use of capital letters, layout and paragraphing is incalculable.

Unless they are already very experienced, staff who are given the task of writing the first draft also need specific instruction but it takes them a long time before they acquire the necessary expertise. Every separate thought needs a new paragraph. Sentences must be short. A complicated or unusual word should not be used when a normal English word can convey the meaning. Finally, the text on each topic or subject should end with a short, clear conclusion or recommendation, the reasons for which flow naturally and obviously from the text which precedes it. If these conclusions or recommendations are all brought together at the end of the report, the reader can go through them quickly and form a clear idea about the main points. If he wishes to pursue any one of them in detail, he can refer back to the text to study the argument.

Even the index requires expert staff. We tried to write it ourselves on the Royal Commission, but soon gave it up and employed skilled persons who are paid to do it as a separate task. The first draft index had some strange entries. Chapter 35 dealt with the dull subject of discrimination of race or sex in the legal profession, and this is what the draftsman made of it; his mind seems to have been dwelling on subjects which the Commission had overlooked:

sex
    cessation of, 35.5
    conclusion on evidence received, 35.19
    definition, 35.4
    evidence of, 35.17-19
    extent of, 35.17-19
    governing bodies, women members, 35.14
    guidance to heads of chambers, 35.21
    information to potential entrants, 35.28
    machinery to combat, recommended, 35.22
    'maternity leave' recommended, 35.25
    number of women in profession, 35.8-14
    offices and chambers, in, 35.15
    refresher courses for women, 35.27
    remedies for, 35.21-30
    statistics relevant to, 35.8-14
    women benches, 35.14, 30
    summary of considerations, 35.46

5.

Other Activities

My dedication to the firm and pressure of work did not prevent me from having outside interests in my leisure time. I digress for a page or two to explain how I relaxed because if I had not done so I am sure I would have collapsed with some sort of breakdown due to stress and overwork. Indeed, in the early 1950s there were signs of a breakdown but, with my wife's support, I overcame the problem.

Later in my life, a friend who had occasion to review my curriculum vitae commented that it reminded him of Mark Twain, who said in his eighth decade: 'I have achieved my seventy years in the usual way: by sticking strictly to a scheme of life that would kill anyone else.' I played tennis and golf regularly, but never achieved more than a modest ability in either. At the age of 48, I came to the conclusion that, with increasing years, it was foolish to run about the tennis court furiously at weekends and sit on an office stool all the week. I therefore gave up tennis and took to sailing. I found that I could do this at Itchenor, near Chichester, which was within reach of my home in Surrey. At Itchenor, and at some other ports in the Solent, keen racing took place every weekend in the X-one design class. It is a small, half-decked sloop with a heavy keel and is a suitable vessel for the middle-aged who cannot go ocean racing for several days on end. I have raced there ever since with occasional success and it has given me both pleasure and relaxation. I have also been keen on shooting. Before I left South Africa I had learned to use a shotgun and I hoped sooner or later to be able to do so in England. D'Arcy Cooper was a keen sportsman and in 1929 he bought an estate in Sussex called Drovers and I was often allowed to shoot with him.

In the 1930s, the risks caused by Hitler's rise to power

were foreseen but it was hoped that war could be avoided if we could establish good relations with Germany, both industrially and in the diplomatic field. The organisation which was set up for the purpose was called, if I remember rightly, the Anglo German Fellowship and D'Arcy Cooper was one of many who persevered in this field. Dinners were held at which leaders of both countries in different fields of activity (including sport) could meet. I was taken on one occasion as a guest but I got the impression that there was no genuine or instinctive warmth in the contacts which both sides hoped to develop. C B Fry of cricketing fame was at our table. At the end of dinner a huge effigy in ice, about six feet long, was wheeled in portraying emblems of both countries locked, or rather frozen, in amity together. C B Fry looked up for a moment and said, 'Ah, *l'entente glaciale'*, and resumed his conversation. It expressed in two words the doubts which deep down permeated the Anglo German Fellowship despite the outward displays of *bonhomie*.

Another approach was through the German ambassador who at that time was Joachim von Ribbentrop. D'Arcy used to invite him down to shoot in Sussex and join a house party. The women in the house party liked von Ribbentrop: his manners were punctilious, he would click his heels and kiss the hands of the ladies when he met them or said goodbye and he was attentive as a guest. The men disliked him because they felt that he was bogus. Soon after we sat down to dinner each evening the butler would announce that there was a telephone call for the ambassador. Von Ribbentrop would get up, murmuring ostentatiously 'the Fuehrer' and disappear for ten minutes. We came to the conclusion that this was a piece of play acting and that the call was from a secretary at the German embassy in London. After the war von Ribbentrop was tried as a war criminal and hanged. I have never felt comfortable about the Nuremburg war trials tribunal and, much as I despised von Ribbentrop, did not feel that he was the sort of character who merited hanging. He faced his end with dignity.

When D'Arcy died in 1941 he left the Drovers estate in Sussex to the National Trust but provided that I should have the shooting rights there for my lifetime. I could not afford to take these up until 1951 but since then I have run a shoot there for my family and personal friends and this has been one of the pleasures and relaxations of my life. This year is the sixtieth year, on and off, that I have shot over the ground so that I could find my way round blindfold. The country on the Sussex Downs is unequalled and it is a joy to be there whatever the weather or time of year. Beaters are needed to drive the game over the guns and many of them are drawn from the local villages and we now have grandchildren of men whom I knew as beaters when they were young.

A beater told me of a valuable homely remedy. He said that when he was a boy (he is now about 83) he regularly wet his bed. His mother was much disturbed and eventually consulted an itinerant gypsy who prescribed a certain remedy. She said catch a mouse and give him a raw mouse sandwich. His mother complied with this startingly simple piece of advice and the boy ate it. He said that he never wet his bed again. With advancing years I may be faced with the same problem but I hope that the prospect of a raw mouse sandwich will help to keep me continent.

The keeper who was there when I took over in 1951 was Ted Saint, a well-known character in the district and a keeper of exceptional talents. We were the same age and had known each other all our lives; he was one of my greatest friends. During the War he was a gunner on merchant navy ships and was twice torpedoed. On the second occasion the survivors were loaded into life boats and the German submarine commander pointed in the direction they should row to reach the mainland. It was typical of Ted that he had concealed two pieces of equipment about his person – a gun and a compass. He told me later that he could have shot the submarine commander without any difficulty and that his finger itched, but he felt that the weight of armament against him was too heavily in favour of the submarine. He did, however, set the boat's course by compass and in a quite different direction and after some days they reached Mozambique. As he and his co-survivors were walking down the main street on Lourenço Marques in rags and tatters, a man asked them what they were doing. He was a well-known South African who owned a chain of department stores in South Africa and, after hearing the story, he took them to the local branch and fitted them all out from top to toe. In due course they were all repatriated.

I have always enjoyed working with my hands and ever since I was married I have kept a workshop where I could do some form of woodwork. My skills are limited but I have put together a number of simple pieces which have found their way into my own home or those of my children. My children also find me useful as an unpaid repairer or jobbing carpenter and odd jobs are brought down for me to cope with as best I can. I mention this because woodworking is a splendid therapy. It needs concentration and gives job satisfaction; worrying professional problems are put out of mind.

From time to time my talents have been sorely tested. When I was in Hong Kong in 1986 on the Carrian case (described in Chapter 12, pages 204-210) I was given models, in miniature, of all the the instruments used in a Chinese orchestra. They are beautifully constructed in jade and when I got home I made a wooden wall cabinet in order to display them. I was told at the time that a set had been given to Mrs Thatcher when, as Prime Minister, she visited Hong Kong in 1982 in connection with the proposed transfer of the colony to the Sovereignty of China in 1997. In 1988 I sat next to the Prime Minister at dinner and, in conversation, said I thought we both had a set of these Chinese miniatures. She said that this was true, but she had not known what to do with them and they were still in the box. My host then intervened and said he was sure that I would make a cabinet in which they could be displayed properly.

Cabinet making is a bit up-market from my normal output. However, I set about the task of making an octagonal cabinet in teak, with a silk background and concealed lighting which was duly delivered to Downing Street. It involved many hours of work and gave me a good deal of pleasure in trying to put it together in sufficiently good shape to justify its destination.

It would be wrong to finish an account of my life in Coopers without mentioning the help I got from the distaff side. Some years ago I wrote an article for the information of my partners in the course of which I described the responsibilities of the senior partner's wife. It said this:

> The senior partner's wife is an important cog in the whole machinery. She is on call at all times to attend functions, to entertain overseas partners and their wives (and sometimes their former wives) and often their children who are here for study or other reasons. She must like people and enjoy meeting and entertaining them because entertaining undertaken as a duty is soon detected and resented. She must go overseas with her husband and be able to fit into these diverse surroundings easily and without appearing to patronise. The senior partner and his wife must keep up an establishment in the United Kingdom which enables them to entertain clients and overseas partners in a reasonable, but not ostentatious, way.

On my retirement in 1975 my wife was asked by the firm to write her side of the story and I reproduce the article below. The last sentence sums it all up.

BAG AND BAGGAGE
JINNY BENSON

Looking back on my life I am amazed how often we take rather momentous decisions in the most unlikely places. I had no idea at the time that plighting my troth to Henry, in that most unromantic of places – a London taxicab bound for King's Cross station where I was taking a night sleeper to Scotland – was going to involve me in becoming 'The Baggage'; but so it has turned out. Over the years as a Coopers' wife, and latterly as a C & L wife, I learned what it was to be taken about in a variety of transport – planes, cars, taxis, camels, river boats, ocean liners, trains, rickshaws and on foot.

Bag and baggage! Looking up the words in the *Oxford Dictionary of English Etymology* we find 'bag' – a small receptacle of the sack kind; 'baggage' – portable property, impediments (thirteenth century), rubbish, refuse (though here the dictionary remarks that 'rubbish and refuse are obsolete' – what an escape!). Alas, worse is to follow – worthless woman (sixteenth-century Shakespeare), saucy, silly flighty young woman (seventeenth century).

In the course of that relatively short taxi journey, having said 'yes', HAB instantly outlined for me what the priorities in his life were, and unlike the alphabet C (Coopers) came before B (baggage). Happily at such times we are not wholly rational and so I accepted my husband and his conditions blithely. In September 1939 we were on the brink of war and much larger issues which affected both our lives radically. Henry, having joined the army, was away a great deal so I became used to living for long periods without my husband, which I now recognise as good training for any accountant's wife, especially if he belongs to an international firm.

It was five years and three children later that HAB returned to City life. My first trip as 'the baggage' took us to Cairo where we stayed at the world-famous Shepheards Hotel, remembering not to eat salad or any fruit with skins on, and being advised by a Cairo resident of many years' standing of the inadvisability of drinking large quantities of liquid, however thirsty during the heat of the day. This was long before air-conditioning; it was rattan blinds, electric fans, wide verandahs and dark bedrooms.

These were the years when the international firm was being built up. We soon began fairly regular travels to the USA – New York and Boston (so different from each other), San Francisco, Detroit, New Orleans, to mention but a few of the cities we visited in that great continent. Thus we began to forge the links of friendship which still remain today.

Of course, it was not permitted to know exactly what was happening; one of the things I had been told on that taxi ride was that no firm matters could ever be discussed. I met wives and husbands at dinners, lunches, cocktails, at country clubs and yacht clubs and became skilled in assessing how things were going without any direct information. Inevitably there were dramas, moment of tension and anxiety. I am amazed that, although I was never given any details, I seemed to develop a sort of sixth sense and came to recognise the skills which are necessary if firm and trusting partnerships are to be built on strong foundations.

Canada from coast to coast, the unbelievable flatness of the prairie, apart from the visual impact, indelibly imprinted on my mind when, in the train going from Banff to Vancouver in a glass-topped carriage where we could gaze up at the heights of the Rockies as we wound our way through them. An old Manitoba farmer, looking up with wonder at the mountains – something he had never seen before – remarked, 'But how does the snow stick?'

Australia with all the diversity and energy of a new nation finding itself. For me the excitement of discovering their writers, artists and musicians. When we first went to Sydney the trams were still running down Castlereagh Street past the old Australia Hotel, now pulled down. It had immense character and coming from England, where we were already beginning to be much more casual in our sartorial habits, the hats and gloves of the lunching Australian ladies took me back to my mama's lifetime. Sydney Harbour, the Bridge, those bays seething with boats in the evening and at weekends. Sunday sails with March Hardie to Quarantine Bay and the same lunch that never varied over the years! The Opera House and all that went into its eventual construction in 1974. Melbourne with its excellent Art Gallery where I spent a morning backstairs being shown their collection of Blake drawings and saw how they 'washed' their prints. Perth which we watched grow over the years, from the first visit when we spent a remarkably wet Easter weekend in a hotel with a corrugated iron roof on to which the rain thundered relentlessly, to our last when we arrived at 3 am at the hotel to be greeted and taken to our rooms by a tail-coated gentleman who might have spent all his life at the Ritz in Paris; the land reclamation and what I think must be one of the loveliest university campuses in the world.

New Zealand and our first taste of hotels where one ate early in the evening and shared tables which gave me the opportunity to make some good friends, including a young couple whom I visited twice on return trips – the husband had been ADC to General Slim during the War; Rotorua and the Maoris' haunting music and dancing. On our first trip to Singapore we stayed at Raffles Hotel which was redolent of the past. Now we stay at Hiltons or Inter-

Continentals where the wastepaper baskets are all the same and the rooms alter little except for the prints on the walls; you could be anywhere in the world when you open your eyes in the morning. But, of course, the bath water is hot and room service works – more or less – and the sheets are clean; which reminds me of a wonderful hotel we stayed in at Luxor on the Nile where we had the most beautiful, if shabby, brass bedsteads and two large hand basins with ornate brass taps out of which no water flowed; you were lucky if the plug pulled in the WC down the dark corridor. On the bedroom balcony I stood as dawn was breaking gazing down at a black-clad figure of an old crone gathering twigs to light her morning fire.

The Hiltons and Inter-Continentals mean that we commute between the big cities of the world, we no longer travel; and in our commuting we scarcely have time to take in the fact that we are away from our own country. But differences of sight, sound and language remain. Thankfully, not even hotel builders or accountants can make the world uniform – with no disrespect to International Accounting Standards.

One particularly vivid instance – the office in Bangkok where we attended the official ceremony of blessing by Buddhist monks. All desks and furniture moved back, a large sheet spread on the floor where they sat to receive food. Then they ranged themselves, sitting cross-legged in front of a white-and-blue embroidered cushion propped up against the wall, each holding a stiff oval fan with a long wooden handle, on which was painted, I imagine, each one's 'mantra'. The rest of us were barefooted and kneeling opposite them. Henry poured water from a jug into a basin held by a monk while they chanted and we bowed our heads yoga fashion sitting back on our heels between times. Finally a procession went round each of the rooms before they returned to sit once again and gifts were presented. I was permitted to give one which could only be received by the monk taking a silk scarf from a pocket in his saffron robe and placing it on the ground in front of him; upon this I placed my gift. No monk may receive a gift from the hand of a woman. This made me ponder on the letter and the spirit of the law! The gifts, which were in round wicker baskets, consisted of most practical things – cigarettes, soap, washing powder and toilet rolls and matches. The monks rely entirely, for everything, on what they receive from people and it is quite a common sight in the street to see passers-by pressing gifts into the hands of a monk as he walks through the city. Another moment I remember is of a Rock Temple near Ipoh, of the small gifts of fruit and grain set in bowls before the Buddha, of the simplicity and sincerity flowing from the silent lay figures prostrating themselves in prayer.

Africa, that wonderful continent which has bewitched me from the moment I set foot on her – such a variety of people and places. The part of the world which, as I write, is filling the Western nations with a deep sense of anxiety for all her people, black and white. Strangely, I feel that Africa may be the part of the world which will show us new visions of understanding in relationships. But it will need wisdom and insight on the part of many, if indeed a holocaust of major magnitude does not engulf it and lay waste much of the effort, love and caring, as well as the mistakes, on the part of many people which have gone into bringing Africa and her people to a new dimension of living. The courage and fortitude of what are called expatriates which sounds such a denigrating word; the people who live in a country other than their own, widely different in race and custom. The people who have said, 'This country has given me much, I will stay in the hours of change', and like Ruth in the Bible, 'My ways shall become thy ways.'

Nairobi, the New Stanley Hotel with its thorn tree growing larger each year through the glass roof of the Thorn Tree Café where I sat watching the world go by. A tall Masai tribesman who appeared walkng steadily with his long staff, his blanket thrown over his shoulder, gazing straight ahead, apparently oblivious of the milling crowds of modern Africa around him. We saw him quite some time later on our way to the airport, still striding along.

Salisbury, with its wide, wide streets built, on the insistence of Cecil Rhodes, so that a span of oxen drawing their wagons could turn with ease. Rhodesia has given me my collection of soapstone African carvings which have altered perceptibly over the years till our last visit when in Bulawayo at the Mzilikazi Art Centre I saw work as sophisticated as anywhere in the world. Perhaps the one I treasure most – the first one – a bas-relief carved on a piece of slate which was once a tombstone.

In Zambia I remember perhaps most vividly the Kafue river which I've seen from many angles, the first when we stayed at the Queen's House which was built for the Queen Mother when she opened the Kariba Dam, sitting high up on a promontory with the river rushing far below. A comfortable, English-style bedroom, sitting room and dressing room, but the bathroom had a plastic loo seat which was not built for people of HAB's proportions and we had to confess to the housekeeper that it had cracked!

Kinshasa, Zaire, into which we dropped in the Irwins' jet – dropped with such rapidity that the 'G' factor took over and Henry thought he must have suffered a stroke as he found he could not lift his arm off the pad he was writing on.

Swift and all too short stays in the Lebanon and Greece. We had two nights and one day in Beirut and I had to choose between Biblos, the world's longest inhabited city, and Baalbek. I chose the latter and it was a day of wonder and amazement at the temple so high that its very size seemed to put 'man' into a very small dimension beside God or the gods. Then hail and farewell, for me at any rate, to Tehran and a magic carpet two days visiting Persepolis and Isfahan.

Ghana, Angola, Nigeria – it would take a book to write about them. Lourenço Marques where I remember being taken round the town hall and finding in the major's parlour gilded Louis XV chairs. Spying a small label on the back of one I bent down to discover they came from 'Waring & Gillow, Oxford Street, London'. And this is to pass over, but not to forget our visits to South America and Mexico.

Perhaps the funniest episode of all the years, the one on our last visit to Adelaide, Australia, where I was waiting to be picked up.

I was the only person in the hotel foyer when a car drove up to the entrance, the driver waved gaily so out I went and hopped in. It struck me as we drove away that she looked different but, as we had met but briefly before, I was not troubled. We chatted happily and about five minutes later we drew up at a hairdresser's. My driver stopped and looked at me; before she could speak I said, 'Who do you think I am?' 'Dr Waldstein,' she replied. 'Aren't you?' We collapsed with laughter and returned to find that Dr Waldstein, in her turn, had greeted my friend with equal certainty!

Lest it be thought that being 'the baggage' is all first-class air travel, luxury hotels and excitement, let me say something of the other side of the 'portable property'. It means leaving home and children and being constantly on the move, two days here, three days there, often with long flights in between and delays which ate into precious hours of sleep. No time to acclimatise either to weather, time or people. It meant that if brief encounters were going to mean more than polite replies to stock questions ('How long are you staying?', 'Did you have a good flight?') I had to pay attention and listen hard, but you would be surprised at the life stories to which I have listened. All this meant for me the discipline of concentration, something I find very hard; my capacity, unlike my husband's, is very limited. This 'saucy woman' ('the baggage') has been given a wonderful experience of living – not always easy, quite often stressful but, having learned early where best-beloved's commitment lay, I have not too often felt jealous of my rival; indeed she has taught me almost all that I know about relationships, communication, loving, laughing and swearing, all shades of light and dark which make up life and living.

My gratitude in having being able to share in the partnership of Coopers & Lybrand is beyond telling. It has given me so many friends, both old and young; I remember the constant stream of sons and daughters of overseas partners who have stayed with us over the years for Christmas or Easter or any odd night or weekend they wanted a bed, and they still do. My tapestry of life is very full and I know not when it will finish finally, but my overwhelming sense is 'how blessed we have been.'

I retired from the firm in 1975 at the age of 65, which was the retiring age I fixed myself when we introduced a pension scheme for partners some years earlier. The age limit has since been reduced. I had been knighted in 1964 and made GBE in 1971. I do not know which of the work I had carried out merited the knighthood, but the GBE was, I think, awarded after I had spent a good deal of time working on an enquiry into the organisation of the Ministry of Defence, to which I refer later in Chapter 8.

When I was given a knighthood, I thought that I would like to have a coat of arms. A short time previously I had done some work on behalf of the College of Heralds, so I asked Garter King of Arms to design a coat of arms for me. He asked me what motto I wished to use. I said that the instruction I had tried my best to instil into my children was 'Do the job properly'. He found it impossible to translate this into Latin and the best alternative he could find was 'Quod facio valde facio'. According to the dictionary 'valde' means vigorously and energetically. It was not quite the emphasis I wanted but I had to put up with it.

Three professional awards have been made to me. The first was in 1971 by the University of Hartford in Connecticut. The second was election to the Accounting Hall of Fame by the Ohio State University in 1984. I am the only living Englishman who has been elected to it; another Englishman was elected but this took place after his death. The third was also in 1984 and was the Founding Societies' Centenary Award. The Founding Societies were the Societies of Accountants in Liverpool, London, Manchester and Sheffield which were formed before the Institute received its charter in 1880. When the Institute reached its centenary, the four societies decided to make an annual award to a chartered accountant who in their opinion had given special service to the profession.

The award was presented to me by Lord Richardson of Duntisbourne, the former Governor of the Bank of England at a dinner at the Institute. In the course of my reply I spoke rather petulantly and said that I was exasperated by people who concentrated on their 'rights' and the privileges to which they felt entitled. I felt that no one had 'rights' until he had fulfilled his obligations to society which never seemed to be mentioned. I then gave the obligations, or nine principles, which seemed to me should guide the conduct of our profession. It astonished me to realise that, until I came to prepare the speech, I had never put them together before. The Founding Societies and the Institute were also interested in this subject and the nine principles are now part of the written material which is given to every person on admission as a chartered accountant after passing the examinations. They are as follows:

First, the profession must be controlled by a governing body which, in professional matters of accountancy, directs the behaviour of its members. The members for their part, and this is sometimes forgotten, have a responsibility to subordinate their selfish private interest in favour of support for the governing body.

Second, the governing body must set adequate standards of education as a condition of entry and thereafter ensure that students obtain an acceptable standard of professional competence. Training and education do not stop on qualification but must continue throughout the members' professional lives.

Third, the governing body must set the ethical rules and professional standards which are to be observed by the member. These should be higher than those which can be established by the general law.

Fourth, the rules and standards enforced by the governing body should be designed for the benefit of the public and not for the private advantage of the members.

Fifth, the governing body must take disciplinary action, including if necessary expulsion from membership, if the rules and standards it lays down are not observed or a member is guilty of bad professional work.

Sixth, work such as auditing should be reserved to our profession by statute, not because it is for the advantage of the members but because, for the protection of the public, it should be carried out only by persons with the requisite training, standards and disciplines.

Seventh, the governing body must satisfy itself that there is fair and open competition in the practice of the profession so that the public is not at risk of being exploited. It follows that members in practice must give information to the public about their experience, competence, capacity to do the work and the fees payable.

Eighth, the members of the profession, whether in practice or employment must be independent in thought and outlook. They must be willing to speak their minds without fear or favour. They must not allow themselves to be put under the control or dominance of any person or organisation which could impair this independence.

Ninth, in its particular field of learning the profession must give leadership to the public it serves.

One of the pleasures my wife and I have had since retirement from the firm has been the opportunity to keep in touch with former partners and their families worldwide. We are still in continuous touch with many of them in the

United Kingdom and whenever we have been abroad we have called on or stayed with them. Our flat in London is open house to the children and grandchildren of past and present partners abroad, who come to the UK to study or on holiday visits. After a warning letter from a parent or grandparent overseas, it is no surprise to have a telephone call from someone whom we may never have seen before, but who relies on this well-established international network, asking whether he or she may stay with us for a long or short period. It also saves their limited pockets from the crippling costs of living in hotels or digs in London.

6.

Accounting Standards

In the early years of my professional life I thought it was impossible to lay down national standards in accounting matters and I am sure that I did not give international standards a thought. It seemed to me at that time that the wide range of different conditions and circumstances which affected commercial, industrial and financial businesses made any form of uniformity out of the question. Over the years all my opinions – professional, social, religious and political – have changed or been significantly modified, and after the Second World War I began to realise that a degree of uniformity in accounting matters was not only desirable but necessary.

Two things began this change of outlook, both of which I have already described. The first was my experiences in the Royal Ordnance Factories. The second was the realisation that, if the firm was to be able to build up a national and international accounting practice, it would be quite impossible to do so without clear manuals for the guidance of partners and staff, worldwide, who were engaged on professional work. These two experiences opened my eyes; changes were beginning to take shape in other fields.

As peace-time conditions returned, professional accountancy bodies in different parts of the world began to codify the widely differing accounting treatments which were in use in their respective countries and authoritative papers began to be produced. They were called by different names – recommendations, principles, guidelines, opinions and statements. By whatever name, they were the beginnings of what we now refer to as Accounting Standards.

A great deal of time and effort was spent by dedicated men

on this work. By modern standards, some of the papers now look crude, but at the time they were first issued they were up to date and a big advance in accounting thought. There was, however one serious defect. They were prepared without sufficient reference to what was happening in other countries so that authoritative publications were issued in different countries which conflicted, sometimes in minor ways, but sometimes on fundamental points of principle.

Soon after taking office as President of the Institute in June 1966 I visited Canada and the United States and had discussions with the heads of the accounting bodies there. At the annual conference of the Canadian Institute of Chartered Accountants in Regina, Saskatchewan in August 1966, a meeting took place with the President of that Institute and the President of the American Institute of Certified Public Accountants (AICPA). I suggested to them that we should set up a three-nation group to study major accounting problems and to issue an agreed statement upon each of them. We agreed quickly that such an enterprise would be worthwhile.

At the end of September 1966 I met the executive committee of the AICPA which, on that occasion, was meeting in Boston and I set out below a copy of the minute which the AICPA has allowed me to reproduce. Looking back, this minute may have some historical significance as I think it marked a turning point in international relationships in the accountancy profession.

PROPOSAL FOR INTERNATIONAL STUDY GROUP

At the invitation of President Trueblood, Sir Henry Benson of the Institute of Chartered Accountants in England and Wales appeared before the executive committee to present a proposal for the creation of a 'study group' composed of two or three representatives of the English, Canadian and American institutes to organise a programe of comparative studies of current trends in accounting thought and practice in the three countries.

In presenting his proposal Sir Henry observed that most of the three organisations pursued their separate ways with compartively little regard to, or knowledge of, accounting and auditing developments in other countries. He suggested that this was a remarkable state of affairs in view of the fact that accountants in the United States, Canada and the United Kingdom were collectively responsible each year for attesting to the fairness of financial statements involving billions of dollars.

Under the proposal the 'study group' would meet at least once a year in each of the countries in rotation and keep in touch with each other by correspondence in the intervals between meetings. The first task of the 'study group' would be to determine the subject areas for exploration and to devise a pattern for the research reports which would facilitate comparisons between the three countries.

It was suggested that the formation of such a group was a simple and effective way, but not the only way, of promoting international cooperation in accounting and it was agreed that similar groups might be organised with accounting organisations in other countries or that the original group might be expanded to include representatives from other countries in due course.

In concluding his presentation Sir Henry declared that the publications to be issued by the 'study group' might bring about a reassessment of present practices and future plans in the three countries; that they would broaden the minds of all who read them and suggest new lines of enquiry; and that they could prove helpful to the profession of accountants in other nations.

After extended discussion, the executive committee resolved to approve the proposal in principle with the understanding that the Presidents of the three organsiations would hold further conferences to develop a plan for an early implementation of the programme.

It was also the sense of the executive committee that when the proposal had received the approval of the three organisations any public announcement on the formation of the 'study group' would be coordinated between the executive staffs of the organisations.

A day or so later I had the privilege of addressing the whole council of the AICPA which happened to be meeting at that time. No formal resolution was put to the council but the proposals appeared to command its approval.

These meetings in Regina and Boston led to the formation

of the Accountants International Study Group (AISG) which first met in February 1967 and began to publish papers every few months on important topics. AISG was eventually disbanded after the International Accounting Standards Committee had been launched, but during its lifetime it issued twenty authoritative papers which began to shape international thinking in the profession.

The Presidents of the three Institutes knew when the AISG was set up that it might engender some measure of discontent in other countries who were likely to feel that they should have been invited to join, or to contribute to, what would be seen as an international group, formed to speak with authority on accounting subjects. We decided deliberately to risk this criticism. It is difficult enough to get agreement on accounting subjects even within a single nation, and we felt that if this exercise was to get off the ground the maximum number of nations who should initially be involved was three, and they should start with the advantage of all speaking a common language. We all had in mind, as the minute records, that if the AISG proved to be a success other nations might be invited to join later on. There was in fact some comment by other nations who felt they had been left out unreasonably but, as far as I know, this disquiet was not deep-seated, particularly when explanations were given about the practical advantages, if not the necessity, of operating initially with a small group.

In the ensuing five or six years events moved faster. There were a number of scandals or failures in different parts of the world which brought criticism upon the business community and the accounting profession; the public began to demand, *inter alia*, higher and more definite accounting rules; the accumulated labour of the professional bodies in different countries since the end of the War was then beginning to bear fruit in, among many other ways, the issue of clear and precise standards; in 1969 the accountancy profession in the UK formally began the publication of Accounting Standards; international barriers were being continually lowered or removed and this was accelerated in

Europe by developments within the Common Market. By the time the accounting bodies of the world met at the Tenth International Congress of Accountants in Sydney in the autumn of 1972, the mood of the accounting profession had changed. The time was right for another step forward.

The lay reader might express surprise at the slow pace at which events moved but the speed of any advance is relative. For a number of reasons major changes take a long time in the accountancy profession. Professional men by their training and upbringing are conservative in outlook; the business community has to be persuaded and convinced; any major change takes a long time to be absorbed and often involves retraining; the student body usually requires three to five years for qualification and there are administrative problems in introducing new teaching and amending examination syllabuses. My own experience is that the accountancy profession has moved surprisingly quickly both nationally and internationally.

In Sydney, therefore, another meeting of the three nations took place similar to the one in Regina six years earlier and the President of the Institute of the Chartered Accountants of Scotland was also present. On this occasion it was proposed that an international body should be set up which would write accounting standards for international use. As at the meeting in Regina, there was no difficulty in reaching agreement in principle but it was realised that there would be practical difficulties in designing a suitable organisation, in financing the enterprise and in getting the approval of the governing bodies of a number of different accountancy organisations. We agreed to meet again before the end of the year after the representatives present had had time to reflect on the proposal.

I went home from Sydney via New Zealand and America and spent all my spare time in thinking out the practical problems and sketching out some sort of organisation and plan of work. I was not alone in this; others who had been in Sydney did much the same thing so that at our next meeting early in December 1972 in London under the then President of the English Institute, there was a store of collective thought on which to draw; progress was rapid.

We had a good deal of discussion about the proposed founder members. Some of those present proposed different combinations but in the end and without much difficulty it was decided to invite the accountancy bodies of six other nations to join us – Australia, France, Germany, Japan, The Netherlands and Mexico. It would have been easy to have made the number larger but, like the original decision to limit the AISG to three, it was felt that the number of countries would have to be restricted to nine. Anything more was thought to be unworkable and anything less would not be representative from an international point of view. We also had to bear in mind that the annual cost of the enterprise would be not inconsiderable and some accounting bodies, although operating to high standards, could not be expected to find their proportion of the cost involved.

After the initial meeting of the three nations in London, a meeting took place in March 1973 at which five of the other six nations were also represented. By this time the proposals had been prepared in draft form. We decided that we would not employ solicitors to formalise the necessary documentation because if solicitors were employed in London the other nations would inevitably want lawyers in their own countries to express a view. So the representatives of the nine nations did their own redrafting of what subsequently became the Agreement and Constitution of the International Accounting Standards Committee (IASC).

The ultimate result may be open to some technical criticism but the intention of the documents was clear and they have stood the test of time. The objectives remain unaltered. The next meeting took place on 28 June 1973; this was followed by the inaugural meeting on 29 June 1973 at which the Agreement and Constitution were signed by representatives of sixteen accountancy bodies from the nine nations. The Earl of Limerick was also present representing the Department of Trade and Industry of the United

Kingdom. I was appointed chairman of the IASC.

Looking back on these events it is extraordinary that the IASC was set up and in operation only some eight or nine months after the meeting in Sydney. I think the reason was a spontaneous feeling in the accountancy profession that something needed to be done quickly and that it was important to let the public see that action was being taken. I also believe that if the process had been delayed for several months every nation, not least my own, would have discovered flaws or practical difficulties in the proposals and the whole venture would have come to a stop.

When the IASC was formed it was provided that it would promulgate 'basic' standards. I, among others, was responsible for the use of this word. I am not sure precisely what others had in mind at the time, but I meant to convey the impression that the standards issued would be simple and straightforward, on topics that went to the root of published financial statements. I did not envisage highly complicated and sophisticated standards with detailed argumentation explaining all the possible alternatives – of which there are some examples in existence in different countries.

I think this view is borne out by an extract from the paper which was prepared after the meeting of the three nations in London in December 1972 and which indicates what was in mind at the time:

> Such Standards must ensure a significant improvement to the quality and comparability of corporate disclosure and yet be capable of rapid acceptance and implementation worldwide. Such Standards would need to be short, clear and uncomplicated if they were to achieve their purpose.

Indeed, the subjects which we discussed during the formative meetings at the end of 1972 and in the first half of 1973 were the very topics on which Standards or Exposure Drafts were subsequently issued by the IASC – accounting policies, inventory valuation, consolidated accounts, depreciation, the minimum information to be disclosed, and the like.

In my own country, and elsewhere abroad, the role of the IASC and the interpretation to be placed on the word 'basic' were construed by different people in different ways. Some believed that there would be great difficulty in the IASC reaching agreement on any topic, and that any standards which emerged would be unlikely to have much impact. Others saw a more positive role for the IASC but wished to see what emerged in the initial years before passing judgement. The consensus of opinion was that it was a bold experiment which was worth undertaking.

The IASC got down to work on 29 June 1973, the day it was inaugurated. It laid down a programme and timetable which, subject to some not very serious lapses, were adhered to. For the first few months everything went well. Then, as exposure drafts began to be issued it was suddenly borne in on the accountancy profession and the world that the International Standards would have teeth. More than that, under the Agreement and Constitution both founder and associate members were expected to comply with Standards.

In consequence of this realisation national prejudices were aroused; there were complaints that the subjects covered by the IASC were too advanced and were not 'basic'; the exposure drafts were said to be too detailed; the composition of the committee was criticised. It was a difficult time but the sixteen acccountancy bodies which had signed the Agreement and Constitution remained steadfast, despite criticisms. The IASC reassessed its position and stuck to its guns. At the same time a growing body of opinion began to recognise that the purpose behind the IASC was important and should be supported. This was made apparent when accountancy bodies from many other nations, over and above the founder members, applied to join. Not only did they believe that it would help to keep them up to date in relation to international accounting matters but they realised that it would save the heavy cost in time and money of writing standards for their own members. I left the chair in 1976 after three years. The detailed method of operation we adopted when I was in office was as follows. When the full Committee had decided that a particular topic was suitable for an International Standard a steering committee was appointed. Steering committees usually comprised one or more representatives from three countries but occasionally, on difficult subjects, the number of countries was increased. The countries chosen for this purpose were normally two of the nine founder countries and one country which was not.

The steering committees were serviced by the IASC secretariat who prepared a brief of all the relevant standards or pronouncements which were known to be in existence on the selected topic. In the light of this information the steering committee settled a 'point outline' which indicated the general lines on which it intended to present the Standard. This 'point outline' was debated by the full Committee at one of its three annual meetings.

In the light of this debate a preliminary draft of an Exposure Draft was submitted to a subsequent meeting of the full Committee for further comment and debate. A final Exposure Draft was then prepared which was examined with meticulous care at a further meeting of the full Committee held some months later. Normally, after appropriate alteration, this was approved for issue to the public at the latter meeting. In short, the substance of every Exposure Draft was debated by the full Committee on three separate occasions before it was authorised for issue.

The Exposure Drafts had a wide circulation; some countries sent them direct to selected people or firms; for example, about 3,000 copies were so issued in the United Kingdom and 20,000 in the United States. In other countries use was made of the professional journals. In this way every Exposure Draft was drawn to the attention of well over 100,000 people in different countries. The number of comments received in response to an Exposure Draft was relatively small. These comments were collected within the different countries and then forwarded to the secretariat of the IASC in London who reassembled the information in a way suitable for examination by the steering committee. Each comment was considered on its merits to ascertain whether it was relevant and, if so, whether a change in the Exposure Draft was warranted. In a great many cases the comments received were contradictory which did not make the steering committee's work easier.

On the basis of this study by the steering committee the exposure draft was revised and submitted to the full Committee in the form of a definite Standard. This was discussed in detail and, in the light of the decisions then made, the Standard was approved for issue. The Standards were expressed in English and it was the responsibility of each country, if English was not the mother tongue, to prepare and issue translations for local use.

One of the three full Committee meetings in each year was held outside the United Kingdom but the other two were held in London. The steering committees, on the other hand, met in different parts of the world depending on which countries were represented on them. It would be impracticable to dispense with any of these meetings and to conduct the affairs of the IASC by correspondence; it will be apparent, therefore, that the cost is considerable.

The only payments made by the IASC for work performed were to the full-time secretariat. In an age when overmanning is rampant, the IASC's record was clean. The total number of the secretariat was three and it is a tribute to their quality and industry that they were able to cope efficiently with a considerable volume of exacting work in addition to much overseas travel. The men who sat on the IASC were, and are still, leaders of the profession in their own countries. All of them had to travel many thousands of miles to sit on steering committees and to be present at the main Committee meetings. The paperwork is technical and exacting. One of the most heart-warming experiences of my professional life was the objective and unselfish work that the members devoted to the task. The cost in money was considerable but that is the least part of the cost. The cost in unpaid professional and leisure time has been enormous. I doubt whether this effort has been realised or appreciated and I am glad to place it formally on the record.

Changes and improvements in the procedures have, of course, taken place over the years but the care and attention which is given to the preparation of Exposure Drafts and Standards has in no way diminished. The Board which now controls the IASC has been widened to include representatives from thirteen countries and the number of persons who sit on each of the steering committees is larger – usually four or five. Another major improvement has been the appointment of a consultative group representing the users and preparers of financial statements. A factor which will add weight is the work of the International Federation of Accountants (IFAC) which was formed in 1977. This is the international organisation which represents the professional accounting bodies of the world. It has issued, up to the time of writing, twenty-six guidelines on auditing which provide authoritative and complementary guidance for practitioners on that subject. Accounting standards and auditing guidelines go hand in hand and in course of time should help to raise standards worldwide. Both are needed and both must be applied if the standards of the accountancy profession are to be held at the right level.

What then of the future? I believe the IASC has come through its formative years with an enhanced reputation. It is now, in 1989, an accepted part of the accountancy profession worldwide and one hundred accounting bodies in seventy-six different countries are members of it. The individual members of these accountancy bodies represent an overwhelming majority of the trained and qualified accountants in the world today. It should also be remembered that the accounting bodies who are members have between them a very large student body who will be the accountants of tomorrow. At the time of writing twenty-eight definitive Standards have been issued and Exposure Drafts have been issued on a number of other subjects. Many of the smaller nations, who do not have adequate resources of money or personnel to prepare standards, adopt the International Standards more or less verbatim as their own national standards. The need for International Accounting Standards is becoming more widely recognised as each year goes by and the IASC is increasingly in touch with organisations, national and international, which in one way or another are concerned with the integrity of financial statements. In the Carrian trial (referred to in Chapter 12, pages 204-210) I was interested to notice that International Accounting Standards were often referred to for authoritative guidance.

I believe that the main thrust for the future should be in three ways. First, some of the present Standards reflect a compromise and proffer alternatives. I think that those Standards need to be tighter and the alternatives reduced or eliminated. The IASC is conscious of this problem and is taking steps to review the Standards already issued with this in mind. Second, I feel that whenever financial statements are issued to the public they should state whether they comply with International Accounting Standards and, if they do not, the extent to which the Standards have not been observed. Third, although progress is being made, I do not think that any accountancy body anywhere in the world has done enough to ensure that either its own national standards or International Standards are, in fact, being applied by its members in the conduct of their professional practice or in their capacity as directors of business enterprises. It is a heavy and costly operation. It needs a skilled staff to detect failures to comply, and a heavy overhead to follow this up with dispassionate investigation and, if necessary, the imposition of sanctions. This has always been my worry and I pointed out in Chapter 3 that I drew attention to the problem over twenty years ago on the day I was appointed President of the Institute.

If the accountancy, or any other, profession is to command the respect of the public which it serves and which provides it with a living, I believe that it has a duty to do more than write standards. It has a duty to take reasonable steps to see that they are in fact followed. Over and over again, when a company fails or goes into liquidation, the subsequent *post mortem* shows that a contributing factor has been the failure to observe sound accounting standards. In most countries the public is rightly indulgent to professional men, realising that they have a heavy responsibility; errors of judgement are human and are therefore pardoned, but neither the public nor governments will continue to be complacent if clear and authoritative standards are openly disregarded. Standards are written to be observed not to be ignored and the accounting profession should take the necessary steps before the public and governments demand it.

I never thought that the impact of the IASC would be revolutionary or immediate. In meetings and seminars in numerous capitals of the world I have said that the impact would be important in the formative years and of dominating importance in the presentation of financial statements by about the year 2000. The period from the meetings in Regina and Boston to the beginning of the next century is no more than a generation – which is a short period in the lifespan of a great profession – but I am clear beyond peradventure on one issue. The accountancy profession will fall into disrepute and possibly come under government direction unless it ensures that its members comply with its own standards.

I think that this is fully appreciated in the United Kingdom. Early in 1988 the Consultative Committee of Accountancy Bodies set up a committee, under the chairmanship of Sir Ronald Dearing, to review the accounting standard setting process in the United Kingdom, including the methods of enforcement. I gave evidence to the committee in which I expressed the above views with all the conviction I could muster. The Dearing Committee reported later in 1988 and I am glad to see that it laid great emphasis on the need to ensure that in future not only the accounting profession, but also the directors of companies, observe accounting standards and that sanctions will be imposed on those who do not do so. It recommended the continued development of International Standards in the United Kingdom and the Republic of Ireland.

7.

Special Assignments 1946–63

In Chapter 3 I explained that after the last war my firm built a reputation for undertaking investigation work. In this and in later chapters I give a description of some of the tasks which came my way. Most of them were, of course, in the United Kingdom, but sometimes the expertise we had developed was called upon for work overseas.

New Union Goldfields Ltd (South Africa)

In 1947 Norbert Erleigh came to London to try to get a listing on the Stock Exchange for the New Union Goldfields Ltd (NUG), a gold-mining group based in Johannesburg of which he was chairman. He consulted John Todd of the stockbroking firm of Rowe Swann & Co, who said he would be prepared to sponsor the listing provided that I first made an investigation and report into the group's affairs. Norbert Erleigh did not care for the word investigation and between us we settled on the word 'review'.

It turned out that Cooper Brothers & Co in South Africa were the auditors of NUG and I was, in any case, myself a partner in the South African firm. It seemed likely that the work would not be difficult. I sent a manager out from London to begin the 'review' and followed later. When the manager arrived he began looking at the results of the current year which were then under audit and came across some alarming features. On my arrival I was horrified at what I found and it appeared that some massive financial frauds had been carried out during the year.

The manager and I slogged away together for many weeks. I suspected that the locked filing cabinets in the audit room might sooner or later be opened in my absence so I took the precaution of removing all the important documents every night when I went home. The papers I left behind were set in a particular way so that I would know at once whether they had been tampered with. The cabinets were in fact opened and the papers were disarranged which confirmed my suspicions about the integrity of the company's officials.

In due course I drafted an audit report of extraordinary severity. I had two problems. First, I wanted to know where I stood on the subject of defamation. Second, I wanted confirmation that my assessment of the transactions would be supported by top-grade independent lawyers. There were many such lawyers in South Africa but it seemed safer on security grounds to make enquiries in London.

I cabled London at length on both subjects and got reassuring replies after my partners in London had consulted leading Counsel. In the meanwhile Erleigh, and Joseph Milne, his partner in many of the transactions, got wind of what was happening and both of them attempted bribery. Erleigh took me to lunch and we talked all round the subject for an hour and a half. It was not until I left that I realised he was asking me what terms I wanted to change or suppress the audit report. In this respect history seems to have repeated itself. On reading through some papers written by my great uncle, Ernest Cooper, on his early days in the profession he recorded:

> My first business journey abroad was in 1874 to Hamburg. I had to investigate the accounts of a firm associated with a business liquidating in London. I was sat at a table with a huge but gentle wolfhound under it but only conversation was forthcoming. I was puzzled, not having much experience, but on returning to my hotel I awakened to the fact that I had been pressed to name my price. This was my first and only conscious experience of an attempt to bribe.

Milne was later more direct. He offered me a number of advantages and participations in share deals, together with a

1. Alexander Stanley Benson, the author's father (1930).

2. Sir D'Arcy Cooper, Bart — son of Francis Cooper and the author's uncle. Partner in the firm 1910-23 and Chairman of Unilever 1925-41.

You've done well this week, Benson—you can go round the office and fill all the ink wells

3. *An early step up the promotion ladder.*

4. *HAB and AVB, during the war, at the Guards Chapel, Birdcage Walk at the christening of their eldest child, Peter (1941).*

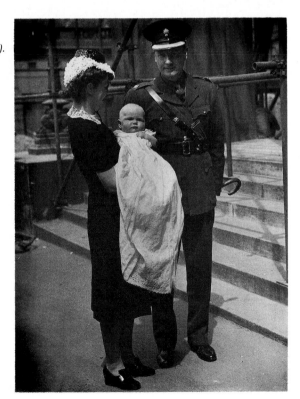

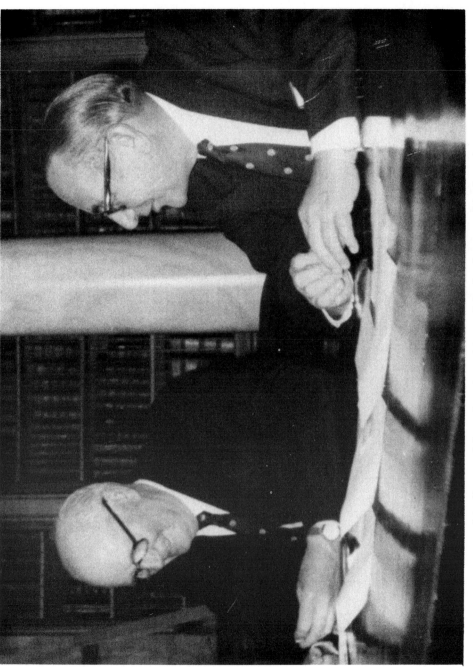

5. John Pears and the author, the architects of the development of the firm after the Second World War.

6. Florence Mary Benson, the author's mother, at the centenary of the firm, flanked by her son and grandson. (Her father, Francis Cooper, joined his brothers soon after the firm began in 1854.) (1954).

7. Peter Benson, shortly after leaving Eton (1958).

8. *The twins, Michael Benson and Phyllida Dare, on their 40th birthday (1983).*

9. *The first eight grandchildren (the ninth followed later).*

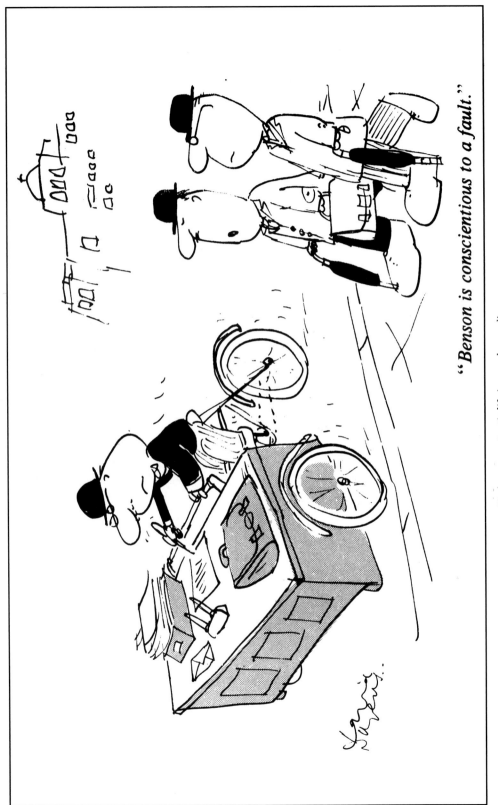

"Benson is conscientious to a fault."

10. *An accountant's life is very demanding.*

11. The birth of International Accounting Standards, Regina, Canada. From left to right: the author, President of the Institute; R L Bamford, the retiring President of the Canadian Institute; R M Trueblood, the President of the American Institute of CPAs; and A F Tempelaar representing the Nederlands Instituut van Accountants (1966).

12. *Shooting at Drovers. Paddy Evan-Jones fifth from the left was Secretary of the Institute of Chartered Accountants in England and Wales (1968).*

13. *Recruiting staff for the firm.*

"I must say, Mr. Benson, you make chartered accountancy sound very exciting."

14. HAB and AVB shooting in Scotland at Glen Kyllachy (1972).

15. The International Accounting Standards Committee, comprising representatives from Australia, Canada, France, Germany, Japan, Mexico, Netherlands, United Kingdom and Ireland, and the United States of America (1975).

16. *HAB and AVB shooting in Scotland at Rottal (1977).*

17. *The Royal Commission on Legal Services: Peter Oppenheimer, Darwin Templeton, Ralf Dahrendorf, Max Williams, Sir Sydney Templeman MBE, Peter Goldman CBE, Alwyn Roberts, Mark Littman, John Heritage (Secretary) (Standing); Joe Haines, Sally Ramsden, HAB, Len Edmondson, David Seligmam (Sitting); Susan Marsden-Smedley and Tom Harper (absent) (1979).*

18. 'Place me on Suniums marbled steep'
    AVB with sons, Peter and Michael, and daughters-in-law, Jane and Rachel (1979).

19. *Introduction to the House of Lords with Garter King of Arms (1981).*

20. Rough weather at Cowes (1985).

21. Freedom of the City of London for HAB and AVB (1986).

22. The start of the Safari in Kenya with the children and grandchildren (1987).

23. The dining room at Samburu Camp, Kenya (1987).

24. *A friend we met on Safari, after breakfast. We passed underneath and could have pulled her tail, but it would have been impolite.*

25. *The costliest salmon ever grassed after 52 years, on and off, of failure on the Findhorn river (1988).*

non-executive directorship at £20,000 a year. I said that I could not accept these offers but Milne misunderstood the reply and said that if they were not enough how much did I want?

I was nervous that the publication of the report and accounts bearing this savage audit report might produce a panic on the Johannesburg Stock Exchange so I went to see J H Hofmeyer, the much respected Minister of Finance at the Union Buildings in Pretoria. He was helpful and understanding and was grateful to have been informed so that the government was not taken by surprise. A copy of the audit report may be of interest to some readers who are concerned with the accounts of public companies and it is reproduced below. It should be pointed out that this audit report was written before the words 'true and fair' or 'fairly present' had been enshrined in audit procedure. At that time also little emphasis had been given to window-dressing (see paragraph 7 of the report) or to insider dealing and there was no legislation on these subjects in Britain or South Africa. The money figures in the audit report were South African pounds and shillings which was the currency then in issue.

TO THE SHAREHOLDERS, NEW UNION GOLDFIELDS LTD

We have audited the balance sheet set out on pages 4 and 5. We are unable to grant a certificate in accordance with Section 90 Quat., of the Companies Act 1926, as amended, and we report the following facts and circumstances which have not been explained to our satisfaction and which prevent us from so certifying.

1. The transactions mentioned in sub-paragraphs (a), (b), (c), (d) and (e) of this paragraph were carried out during the year ended 30 June 1947, between the company on the one hand and Mr N S Erleigh and/or Mr J Milne on the other hand, on the instructions of one or both of them without (except as mentioned in sub-paragraph (e)) the authority of the Board, and, so far as we have been able to ascertain, without complying with the provisions as to disclosure of Directors'

interests in Article 107 of the Company's Articles of Association and Section 70 Quin. of the Companies Act 1926 (as amended). Mr Erleigh was a Managing Director throughout the year; Mr Milne was appointed a Director and a Managing Director on 23 December 1946.

(a) Profits, amounting in all to approximately £270,000 which arose on certain share dealings carried out by the Company and which, in our opinion, belonged to the Company, were paid to, or credited to the personal accounts of Mr Erleigh and Mr Milne in equal proportions.

(b) In July 1946, 80,000 shares out of the Company's holding in Corporation Syndicate Ltd were sold to Mr Erleigh and Mr Milne in equal proportions at 5s per share when the quoted market price was approximately 25s per share.

(c) In January 1947, 40,000 shares out of the Company's holding in Natal Portland Cement Co Ltd were sold to Mr Erleigh and Mr Milne in equal proportions at 5s per share and at the same time options (which expire on 30 April 1948 and have not yet been exercised) were given to Mr Erleigh and Mr Milne to acquire a further 80,000 shares each from the Company at 5s per share. No proper consideration appears to have been received by the Company for these options. The shares in Natal Portland Cement Co Ltd were not then quoted on any stock exchange, but the Company had previously paid an average price of 9s per share for its holding and there was a contemporary sale of a small parcel to a broker at 9s per share.

(d) In February 1947, the Company acquired or subscribed in cash for 806 shares of 5s each at par in British New Union Investment Corporation Ltd, out of a total issued capital of that company of 2,006 shares of 5s each. In February 1947, British New Union Investment Corporation Ltd entered into an agreement with an associated company in the New Union Goldfields group, Union Free State Coal and Gold Mines Ltd, under which it is entitled to receive, in certain events described in the agreement, a royalty of 2½d for every ton of coal extracted and sold or removed from the properties referred to in the agreement. On 30 June 1947, the above 806 shares were transferred to Mr Erleigh at cost.

(e) During the year Mr Erleigh borrowed £352,875 from the

Company and Mr Milne borrowed £219,375, in both cases for financing purchases, on their private accounts, of shares in associated companies in the group. Of these sums £31,250 in each case was approved by the Board *ex post facto*. The shares so purchased, the market value of which on 30 June 1947 was respectively £780,844 and £362,969, were, and are still, deposited with the company. A large part of these borrowings is still outstanding.

2. On the instructions of Mr Erleigh or Mr Milne sales of shares have been made by the Company to certain persons, including relatives of Mr Erleigh and Mr Milne and members of the staff of the Company, at prices substantially below either their current quoted market prices or the prices at which sales of similar shares were made to third parties. The differences in prices on these transactions during the year to 30 June 1947 amounted in total to approximately £12,000.

3. On 17 March 1947, entries were made in the books, the effect of which was that the Company acquired from British New Union Investment Corporation Ltd 14,300 shares in Free State Development Corporation Ltd, at an average cost of £6 9s 4d per share. The quoted market price of such shares at that date was approximately £4 11s 0d per share. Mr Erleigh and Mr Milne were both directors of British New Union Investment Corporation Ltd and on 17 March 1947 they each held 400 shares out of a total issued capital of that company of 2,006 shares of 5s each. We have not had produced to us either a minute of the Board of New Union Goldfields Ltd, or documents in support of this transaction which, so far as we have been able to ascertain, was carried out without complying with the provisions as to disclosure of Directors' interests in Article 107 of the Company's Articles of Association and Section 70 Quin. of the Companies Act 1926 (as amended).

4. The company has exceeded by a considerable amount the borrowing powers authorised by Article 99 of the Articles of Association.

5. In the light of the information at present available, the shareholding in companies which are not quoted amounting to £1,884,412 cannot, in our opinion, be realised at the present time at the value at which they are shown in the balance sheet.

6. In our opinion the amounts due by associated companies totalling £1,851,906 cannot be realised at that value. We are

further of opinion that a large part of the amounts so due can only be realised over an extended period as the monies have been invested by the associated companies in fixed assets, or are required by them for working capital.

7. Shortly before and on 30 June 1947, the Company caused associated companies in the group to transfer to its banking account cash balances held by those companies. The effect is to increase very largely the balance of cash shown in the balance sheet with a corresponding increase in the liabilities shown as due to associated companies. Similar transfers were made in the previous year.

8. In our opinion proper books and accounts have not been kept in respect of the Riviera Hotel and Country Club.

Roberts, Allsworth, Cooper Brothers & Co
Chartered Accountants (SA)
Auditors

Johannesburg
10 November 1947

Note A report had also had to be made, under the Companies Act, on the profit and loss account and this is contained in the following two paragraphs:

We are unable to make the report on the above accounts as required by Section 90 Ter. of the Companies Act 1926 (as amended), by reason of the facts and circumstances contained in our report on the balance sheet set out on pages 2 and 3, and the following additional matter.

Satisfactory explanations have not been furnished to us as to the reason for charging against the Company the payments made and legal costs incurred in settlement of claims against Mr N S Erleigh personally, amounting to £45,669.

In due course the accounts, with the foregoing audit report, were published. They caused, of course, banner headlines in the press in South Africa and in some financial papers in London. Erleigh and Milne were arrested and brought to trial. I later was asked to give evidence at the trial before a judge and two assessors because, in trials of that nature, the jury system does not apply in South Africa. On and off I spent eleven days in the box but my attendance was not continuous. The defence Council had let it be known that they intended to crucify me in the box but when it came to the point they could not find a great deal to attack me about. I remember one piece of cross examination. I had said that I had had some difficulty in carrying out this investigation and 'had borne the heat and burden of the day'. Counsel said, 'What do you mean by that?' I said, 'I have borne threats, abuse, cajolery, obstruction, attempts at bribery and queer Counsel's opinions.' At that point a member of the public at the back of the court shouted, 'Well done!' The judge made no comment and cross examination by that Counsel ceased soon afterwards. Erleigh and Milne were convicted but they appealed. The appeal was dismissed and they both went to gaol for a term of years.

The case had the effect of laying down certain principles which had not always been understood or appreciated in South Africa in the conduct of financial and commercial affairs. The judgement given in Johannesburg in May 1950 by Judge Lucas and later the judgement of the Supreme Court in Bloemfontein had a profound influence on business in South Africa and the stand taken by the firm in its capacity as auditors strengthened the position of the profession in that country.

While I was in Johannesburg I also gave evidence to a Commission under the chairmanship of Judge Millin which had been set up to consider changes in the company law, in the course of which I dealt with some of the matters which had been brought to light in the NUG case. Further company legislation was shortly afterwards introduced in South Africa and many of the provisions then made were traceable to the events which the NUG case had brought to light.

History has a way of repeating itself. When I was engaged on the Carrian case in Hong Kong in 1987, some forty years afterwards (described in Chapter 12) I had occasion to give evidence in court setting out the nature of the audit report which I thought should have been issued by the auditors of the Carrian company on the accounts for the year 1981. The draft was an audit report of extraordinary severity and, if it had been issued in that form, would have created a major crisis in the affairs of the Carrian group and brought some unsatisfactory operations to an end. Prosecuting Counsel, Lionel Swift QC, said to me in conference, 'I can't believe that you have ever issued a report of this type on the accounts of a public company.' I told him that I had indeed done so and recounted, by way of example, the events in the NUG case. Lionel Swift was immediately interested because he thought that the point might arise in the course of my cross-examination. Cables and telex/faxes to Johannesburg were exchanged and within a day or two we had received in Hong Kong a copy of the NUG audit report issued in 1947. It was never in fact used in the Carrian case, but it gave comfort to counsel to know that there was at least one precedent which could be drawn upon if the need arose.

The Overseas Food Corporation – The 'Groundnuts Scheme' (East Africa)

In 1949 in conformity with the policy of the government of the day of national, as opposed to private, ownership a number of large public corporations were formed to control the basic industries or to undertake development projects. One of these was the Overseas Food Corporation, which was designed to exploit the agricultural resources of the Empire in order to provide food for the United Kingdom and, particularly, to grow groundnuts in East Africa. The venture was usually referred to as the 'Groundnuts Scheme'. The decision to grow groundnuts was due to a post-war report which had forecast a world shortage of oil, and the government considered it advisable to undertake a large-scale venture which would help to alleviate a potentially dangerous situation. In fact, the projected shortage did not take place and, as will be seen, the groundnuts scheme did not produce any oil at all.

A four-man team had been sent out to East Africa to find out whether the scheme was feasible and they reported favourably. The Corporation got under way in due course and cleared a huge number of acres of bush where groundnuts were planted during the rainy season. The main area was at a place called Kongwa in Tanganyika as it was then called (now Tanzania). The firm had been appointed auditors and I went out to survey the position and plan the audit in conjunction with our firm in East Africa which had been established in 1947. The soil at Kongwa was a rich red colour, but it had a strange clinging quality. When my white shirts were washed on my return to London it was impossible to get them clean and they had to be discarded. The groundnuts grew well but when the time came to harvest them in the dry season they could not be lifted out of the ground. The red soil, though fertile, was rock hard, and the crop had to be left in the ground.

Before the Second World War that part of East Africa had belonged to Germany. It was rumoured on the scheme that the original survey team had been fortunate in finding charts and records prepared before the War by highly skilled German agronomists. The charts listed the crops, including groundnuts, which would be suitable for planting and the story goes that this discovery influenced the survey team in arriving at their favourable conclusions. Unfortunately it was not discovered until too late that the endorsements on the charts were the crops that would *not* be suitable for planting. I cannot vouch for the veracity of this story but, in the light of events, it has the ring of truth.

I was disturbed on my visit to East Africa to discover the state of the Corporation's books and records. They were clearly in a mess and with the limited trained personnel available on the scheme there was no hope of getting them in order. I came to the conclusion that we would have to qualify our first audit report to the effect that proper books of account had not been kept. This duly occurred and reasons were briefly set out. These qualifications and the enormous margin by which the costs of the scheme exceeded the original estimates drew pubic attention to the folly of proceeding hastily with an ill-designed scheme. A storm of controversy arose in the press and the House of Commons which led to a reorganisation of the affairs of the Corporation and radical changes in the administration. When the accounts of the Corporation were examined by the Committee of Public Accounts of the House of Commons, I was called as the first witness in order to explain not only the circumstances which had led to such a serious qualification of the audit report, but also the position of independent auditors in relation to government corporations. It is believed that this was the first occasion on which professional auditors were called upon by the Public Accounts Committee to give evidence concerning the conduct of a public corporation.

The firm was later appointed by the Corporation to reorganise its financial administration, but the scheme as a whole was a dismal failure. The initial studies had not been sufficiently penetrating; the planning was inadequate and the general administration of the scheme was second rate, made worse by a shortage of trained and competent staff who were capable of working in the primitive conditions prevailing in the area. In the firm we were disturbed by the crudity with which the scheme had been planned and implemented. We therefore wrote a paper with the ponderous title 'Matters to be Considered before a Major Scheme of Colonial Development is Undertaken' which explained the need for careful planning and listed the numerous matters to be taken into account before there was any prospect of launching a successful scheme of this nature. I do not think that the paper had much effect in Whitehall if for no other reason that we began to shed our colonial possessions very soon afterwards; moreover the groundnuts scheme did not inspire the UK government of the day to indulge in any similar enterprises.

The paper emphasised, *inter alia*, the number of different contingencies which have to be taken into consideration and for which provision must be made in the financial estimates. Even after all the known or suspected contingencies have been taken into account, there is a need for a generous unallocated overall allowance. A particular reason for this is that virtually every unexpected event that happens is adverse whether it be floods, hurricanes, strikes, disease, changes of government policy, technical break-downs, delays by subordinate suppliers, or any of the many other difficulties which Mother Nature or the gremlins impose. In examining estimates or forward plans for any large-scale exercise the firm has accordingly always included an overall contingency allowance of not less than 15 per cent. It is seldom excessive and is often inadequate. The experience which the firm gained from this scheme was subsequently to prove of great value when it was called in to assist at the planning stage of other ventures such as the Kariba Dam and hydro electric project, the Volta River project and the Indus Basin scheme.

The Holt Case

In 1948 a dispute arose beteen the Estate Duty Office and the executors of R L Holt about the value of a minority holding of shares he had owned in a private limited company called John Holt & Co (Liverpool) Ltd, which carried on business as traders and merchants in West Africa, mostly Nigeria. The case was important, not only to owners of shares in private companies, but to the accountancy profession, which often has to value shares or agree an appropriate price for shares in private companies with the Revenue authorities.

After a long correspondence between the executors and the Estate Duty Office, in which I took no part, agreement could not be reached and the case reached the High Court in 1953. I was then asked, as an independent accountant, to give evidence on behalf of the executors.

The formula laid down in the Act was: 'the price which . . . such property would fetch if sold in the open market at the time of the death of the deceased.'

The executors contended that the correct basis of valuation was the price at which the shares would have been quoted on the date of death if they had been listed on the Stock Exchange, less a discount because of the difficulty of realising a small number of shares in a private company. The corollary of this was that the value of the shares should be based primarily on the dividends which had arisen and might be expected to arise. Asset value could not, of course, be ignored, but it was of less importance. The business had a considerable volume of assets, but the profits were subject to wide fluctuations, especially in the uncertain trading conditions post-war. The directors had to restrict dividends because a private company does not have ready access to the capital market and cash had to be preserved in the business.

The Crown took a more optimistic view about the company's profits and dividend prospects, and I am satisfied in my own mind that they were influenced unduly by the asset value of the shares. The difference in the valuations was therefore considerable. The executors had originally proposed a price of eleven shillings and threepence. The Crown had started with the price of £3 per share, but later made a formal 'determination' of thirty-four shillings, followed by a further reduction to twenty-five shillings per share which was made shortly before the case was opened in Court.

The case for the executors was entrusted to Brian MacKenna QC (later Sir Brian MacKenna, a High Court judge), who conducted it brilliantly. The Crown case was led by the Solicitor-General, Sir Reginald Manningham-Buller QC. When he was in practice, Manningham-Buller could be rough with witnesses. He was sometimes referred to by his colleagues as Sir Bullying Manner and it proved to be so in this case.

Preparation before the trial is the secret of success in any litigation, civil or criminal. In the Holt case there were five witnesses for the executors and four for the Crown. The case for the executors had been carefully prepared, the witnesses knew the contents of their proofs of evidence which covered the ground thoroughly, and their evidence made a convincing story. The evidence of the Crown's witnesses was at times inconsistent.

After I had given evidence, Manningham-Buller started to cross-examine and produced, for this purpose, a typewritten statement of several pages summarising the Crown's case, which we on our side had never seen before. I had only a few seconds to glance at it when it was handed up to me in the box, but I saw at once that, apart from some embellishments, it was a rehash of all the material which had been included in the Crown's correspondence with the executors in the preceding months. I could quote it almost verbatim and knew by heart the weak arguments which had been incorporated in it.

When Manningham-Buller began his questions, a dialogue on the following lines ensued:

HAB: This document is a mixture of fact and propaganda.

MB: (aggressively) You describe the document as propaganda.

HAB: That is not what I said. I said it was a mixture of fact and propaganda.

I then began to point out some of the passages which I claimed were propaganda.

MB: Have you seen this document before?

HAB: No.

MB: Are you sure?

HAB: Yes. It's your document.

Manningham-Buller was upset. He could not understand how I could pull to pieces a document which I had never seen before and (deliberately) had not been given an opportunity to study. He consulted his supporting team, who confirmed that I could not have seen the document. The result was that his major piece of armament was not of much use to him, and his manner became increasingly aggressive.

At the end of that day, the junior counsel acting for the Crown said he wished to withdraw because he was unwilling to be involved in a case which was being conducted like a murder trial. Later on Manningham-Buller announced in Court that he was bringing in reinforcements to help him, in the shape of a Chancery Silk, but this appointment was too late to repair the damage.

After a hearing of several days, Mr Justice Danckwerts fixed the price of the shares at nineteen shillings, as against my valuation of seventeen shillings and twopence. In modern currency the figures are 95 pence and 85 pence respectively. The executors felt that this was a very satisfactory outcome having regard to the Crown's original claim of £3.

Manningham-Buller was later made Attorney-General and subsequently became Lord Chancellor, when he adopted the name and title of Viscount Dilhorne. There is an oft repeated story about his appointment. It was the practice of an ageing and respected member of the Bar to write politely to any members of his Inn when they received high judicial office, and it is said that he wrote to Viscount Dilhorne on this occasion. Unfortunately he was confused by the change of name, and he concluded his letter with a postcript on the following lines: 'PS: Another agreeable result of your appointment is that it will keep Manningham-Buller out of the job.'

The antipathy between Manningham-Buller and myself, which the Holt case engendered, did not diminish with time. Nearly thirty years later Viscount Dilhorne, as he was then, wrote to me in brusque terms and complained, unreasonably I thought, about a paragraph which appeared in the Report of the Royal Commission on Legal Services; an acidulated correspondence ensued.

The National Coal Board

After the Second World War, when the Labour government was returned to power, the coal industry was nationalised. It was the first great industry in this country to suffer this fate and there were naturally a great many difficulties in the early years in settling the right organisation and arranging for efficient administration. In 1953 the Board appointed an independent advisory committee of five members to examine and report upon the organisation of the National Coal Board. The chairman of the committee was Sir Alexander Fleck (later Lord Fleck), chairman of Imperial Chemical Industries Ltd and I was appointed vice-chairman. At the time the Board employed approximately 780,000 people and operated just short of 900 pits. In 1954 it produced 212 million tons of coal and the financial turnover was over £700 million.

Geoffrey Heyworth, whom I have referred to in Chapter 3 was a non-executive member of the Board. The reason why the committee was set up and the nature of its work were recorded in a memorial volume published on Geoffrey's death, from which this extract is taken.

Heyworth now became the key figure. Helped by Godfrey Mitchell and Hambro he had made a clear and accurate diagnosis of the state of affairs. His capacity and experience enabled him to identify the central issues. He perceived that the direction of the enterprise was bad; that the style of management was misconceived; and that the top management of the enterprise was woefully weak. He knew too that the Board as then comprised could not possible master the situation. It was now that the value of good non-executive directors was demonstrated. Heyworth's abilities enabled him to grasp the essentials within a confused, chaotic situation and to intervene.

It was impossible for him to find the time to effect a cure to the situation himself. But he saw to it that action was taken. The instrument for this was an investigation into the organisation and management of the National Coal Board. He had the powers and status to require this and, no doubt for the same reason, the Advisory Committee on Organisation which was set up included two important members known to him: Henry Benson who was the key figure; and Godfrey Mitchell (who had resigned from the Board because of his dissatisfaction). Godfrey Mitchell with his knowledge of the National Coal Board and his trenchant and uninhibited criticism was a useful member of the committee, knowing the position from inside. Henry Benson was invaluable and his qualities are so well known that there is no need to say more than that he brought them all to bear on the issue. He applied his tireless energy and abilities to it, and was himself largely responsible for the composition of the report. The committee elected Dr Fleck as chairman and the report became known as the 'Fleck Report'. Heyworth, still a member of the Board, was in the background and his wisdom contributed to the thinking of the committee.

The continued talent of those I have mentioned produced a report which was, in the first place, a classic in organisational thinking – the hand of Henry Benson was evident in this. In this aspect the report was, of course, a study of an existing situation, to which it was wholly relevant. It was essentially a correction for the current state of affairs. But it also dealt in a devastating manner with less tangible issues such as the style of management and the divided nature of authority. Some of the more delicate matters, when personalities were the real issue, could not be written into the report in explicit terms but doubtless they were made known to the minister of the day.

When the contents of it became known the minister at first acted properly and robustly: he asked the Board members to place their resignations in his hands. He did not, regrettably, maintain this positive attitude and he did not make all the required changes in membership when a new Board was formed. But it was enough. It was now possible to rectify many of the appalling defects of the situation. The character of the Board and its method of operation had to change.

Credit for the report must largely go to Henry Benson, with some to Godfrey Mitchell. But Heyworth had been the cause of the investigation and an important element in its thinking. It is therefore no exaggeration to say that, in the mid-1950s he saved the National Coal Board from disaster. Many men faced with a situation such as he found would have escaped. Not so Geoffrey Heyworth, though his responsibilities and problems in Unilever would have justified his withdrawal from the Augean stables of the National Coal Board. That would not have been in character. He stayed on to see that they were cleaned up, not resigning until 1955.

Following the publication of the report, the firm was called upon to help the Board to develop model procedures for the provision of planning and control information at all levels of management.

The Balmain Case (Australia)

In 1954 I was asked by our Australian partners to go to Sydney to give evidence on a valuation case. I was asked to do this because, by that time, my firm and I had acquired a good deal of experience in valuation work in the United Kingdom, arising out of the nationalisation of the coal industry and the Holt case. This was my first visit to Australia and I formed an affection for the country which persists to this day. The power station called the Balmain Electric Light Company was being compulsorily acquired by the Electricity Commission of New South Wales and the case turned on the proper compensation payable. I was asked to give expert evidence on behalf of the Electricity Commission. The owners of the power station were represented in court by Garfield Barwick QC (later Sir Garfield Barwick who became Chief Justice of Australia).

The formula in use in the UK for the purpose of the nationalisation of coal was 'willing buyer, willing seller in the open market'. This was used not only for valuing the pits but also for the ancillary undertakings and equipment (including housing) which were attached to the coal-mines. I acted for some coal owners and I was one of the advisers to the Coal Board in fixing compensation for the acquisition of the ancillary undertakings.

The basis of valuation stated in the Electricity Commission Purchase Act 1950 was 'going concern'. The company argued that, on this basis, the value was the depreciated replacement value of the fixed assets, the cost of other tangible assets less liabilities, and in addition a 'going concern' value. This so-called 'going concern' value might have been called goodwill and was loosely founded on estimated future profits. The depreciated replacement value was submitted by the claimants in enormous detail including an inventory comprising a number of volumes.

Evidence on the value of each item in the inventory was given by witnesses for both parties. The company's claim based on this material was A£10 million.

My evidence, given in March 1955, was founded on the principle that a proper basis was net maintainable revenue and a risk rate which was similar to the interpretation placed in the UK upon the formula 'willing buyer, willing seller in the open market'. I expressed the opinion that the depreciated replacement value of the fixed assets was of relatively little importance. My valuation amounted to A£1,990,000 and the judge determined the value at A£2,400,000 which was extremely favourable to the Electricity Commission. The judgement was also important because, for the purpose of a 'going concern' value, it confirmed the soundness of a valuation based on a capitalisation of maintainable revenue at an appropriate risk rate and the rejection of a valuation by reference to the sum of the separate values of each of the physical assets plus a figure of goodwill.

Gar Barwick had a remarkable prestige in those days as an advocate not only in his own country but in London. At that time appeals could be taken from the Courts in Australia to the Privy Council (this has now ceased) and Gar Barwick had a great reputation when he appeared before the Privy Council in London on numerous occasions. He cross-examined me in Sydney for four days and at times our exchanges became heated. There was little warmth in our personal relationship at the end of the case. I met him in London not long afterwards, however, and we formed a firm friendship which exists to this day. He was a keen sailor and I proposed him as a member of the Royal Yacht Squadron at Cowes a few years later. He was also kind enough to come and give evidence to the Royal Commission on Legal Services of which I was chairman from 1976 to 1979. We still correspond two or three times a year and exchange articles and publications on legal and other matters which interest us.

British Transport

In 1960 the Minister of Transport Ernest Marples (later Lord Marples) appointed an advisory committee under the chairmanship of Sir Ivan Stedeford, the chairman of Tube Industries Ltd, to examine the structure, finance and working of the organisation controlled by the British Transport Commission. The Commission was responsible for the operation of British Railways, public transport in London and for certain interests in docks, shipping, canals, hotels and other ancillary activities. It employed over 700,000 people. The other members appointed by the Minister were Dick Beeching (later Lord Beeching), Frank Kearton (later Lord Kearton) and myself. We had 'two observers' in the form of prominent civil servants.

Work on the committee did not start well for me. Soon after we were appointed we made a visit to the north, starting at Euston and we were accompanied by the chairman of the commission, Lord Robertson of Oakridge. While we were waiting on the station platform at Euston, I pointed to the logo or crest which was painted on the side of each railway coach. It was very elaborate and in many colours. I said to the chairman that I could not understand why the railways wasted their money on that type of ornament when there was so much refurbishment needed on the railways system itself. The chairman said, very frostily, 'I designed it myself'.

It was an unhappy committee. Stedeford wrote what he thought the answers should be and he was very put out when his fellow members on the committee disagreed with him. He said in effect that the tradition in such cases was for the chairman to settle the general lines of the report and for the other members to support him. As a result there was a split down the middle. Beeching and I were in agreement on one side and Stedeford and Kearton had different views on the other. A joint report was out of the question. Beeching wrote the bulk of the paper, expressing his views and mine on the steps which we thought needed to be taken to improve a confused and top-heavy administration, and Stedeford and Kearton wrote their own opinions.

This was an embarrassment to the Minister of Transport and none of the papers was ever published. The views were so divergent that it would have merely created public controversy and disagreement and would probably have required another committee to look at the subject afresh. In due course the Government issued a White Paper arising out of the studies which had been made which revised the structure of the Commission and made far-reaching financial changes. The Minister appeared to veer in favour of the views expressed by Beeching and myself; Beeching was appointed to the British Transport Commission in 1961 and made chairman of the British Railways Board in 1963 where he introduced many radical changes and brought into effect large economies of operation. In later years, Beeching was at times a controversial figure but I had a high admiration for him. He had a clear and decisive mind and could express himself lucidly both orally and in writing; in argument he was forthright and convincing.

The Northern Irish Railways

A year later in 1961, on Beeching's recommendation, I was appointed to investigate and report on the position of the railways in Northern Irleand. I think Beeching suggested that I should do the job in an individual capacity because of our earlier experiences on the British Transport Commission. It had the merit of avoiding the risk of a minority or conflicting report. The railways in Northern Ireland were losing money and I think (but was never formally told) that the government of the Province hoped that I would recommend their total closure. While engaged on this work, and before I had come to any conclusions, I paid a visit on business to Boston in America. I stayed a night with some friends outside Boston and we drove into the city by car in the morning. It was a nightmare, and the queue of cars, head to tail, was enormous. I asked whether we could not get in by rail but my host said that the local railway system had been closed down and they had regretted it ever since.

This made me think carefully about Belfast. It is the only large city in the Province and all major activities are concentrated there. At that time the Province had a population of about 1,400,000, of which one half were domiciled in the Belfast urban area. In the light of my experience in Boston, and the dictates of common sense, it seemed to me to be madness to do away with any method of commuter ingress or egress to a large city. Motor cars, buses, railways, water, air and underground trains – all are needed to speed up the movement of people and goods traffic.

One of the witnesses who gave oral evidence was connected with the ferry service operating from Larne to Scotland. I suggested to him that time and expense might be saved if the ferry ships avoided Larne and came directly into Belfast harbour. He looked me coldly in the eye and said with a ring of conviction in his voice, 'If I had a gun I'd shoot you.' This was compelling evidence and in the final report, I did not recommend that there should be any change – but for different and, I hope, more convincing reasons.

My report made suggestions for curtailing some parts of the railway system, which appeared to be redundant, but urged the retention of all the commuter lines in and out of Belfast and also the line to Dublin. I proposed better linkage of the rail systems within the city of Belfast to give greater flexibility. Considerable changes on these lines have come to pass which have proved successful in moving passengers and small goods traffic. I am told that the commuter lines are popular and well patronised.

New Zealand Produce and Shipping

In 1962 the four UK shipping lines engaged in the New Zealand trade and the three produce boards in New Zealand (meat, dairy products and fruit) each set up a committee to examine the possibility of introducing economies in the shipping services; improvements in the procedures and in scheduling the shipping requirements of exporters and importers; and economies from palletisation and methods of loading and discharging cargoes. I was appointed chairman of the shipping committee which sat in London; the produce board committee sat in New Zealand under a different chairman. The two committees were expected to work together to fulfil the terms of reference and, in due course, they produced a single and unanimous report.

This was a formidable task. Briefly the shipping arrangements for the export of New Zealand produce were wasteful and inefficient. Expensive cargo vessels completed only about two round trips to New Zealand and back each year. They called at a number of different ports in New Zealand to pick up small lots of cargo and on each occasion there was a waste of time and expense. The methods of shipping the produce to the ports within New Zealand were wasteful and time-consuming. The systems of loading at the different ports were different and were open to considerable improvement. There was very little coordination of effort and other administrative weaknesses.

I paid visits to New Zealand and visited most of the ports and installations and I did the same thing in the United Kingdom. The chairman of the produce board committee, B R Law, came to London and made similar enquiries here and in New Zealand. We pooled our knowledge and ideas and in the comprehensive report which appeared two years later we covered virtually every aspect of the movement of goods from the point of production in New Zealand to the final destination overseas. Our objective was to try and streamline the process from beginning to the end. The report was packed with statistics which helped to support our recommendations.

These recommendations, when adopted, began to take effect and in reporting on the port operations in 1964 Sir John Ormond, the chairman of the New Zealand Meat Producers Board, said the numbers of ports of call had been reduced, cargo flows had increased by approximately 10 per

cent and an average saving of 560 ship days on the New
Zealand coast had been recorded. He added:

> I do not know of any business reorganisation which has
> yielded such quick results on such a vast scale. It
> represents, however, only a first step on the whole
> 'streamlining' exercise. It is a promise for the future and I
> hope that the thrust is maintained so that this promise is
> fulfilled.

The enquiry served a valuable purpose, but, like all
enquiries of this nature, the full benefit is not only the
recommendations themselves. The enquiry itself makes
everybody think. It causes them to wonder how they can
defend themselves against criticism in the report; to think
how things could be done better; and very often it enables
them to justify, and later get established, changes they have
wanted for a long time but have not been able to achieve on
their own. Since the report there have been further radical
changes in the shipping of New Zealand produce as a result
of the introduction of refrigerated container ships and the
composition of the shipping lines.

Value Added Tax

In 1963 I was on my way back from Australia when the
aeroplane stopped at Tehran because of an engine failure. I
read in an English newspaper that I had been appointed by
the Chancellor of the Exchequer, without my knowledge, to
sit on a committee to enquire into the practical effects of the
introduction of a turnover tax (in effect VAT) either in
addition to, or in substitution of, the existing purchase tax or
profits tax, or both. On return to London I found this
appointment to be true. The chairman of the committee was
Gordon Richardson (later Lord Richardson) and Sir Donald
McDougall, a distinguished economist.

One of the circumstances that led to the appointment of

this committee appeared to be that the economy in Britain was thought to be stagnating, whereas in France and Germany exports had expanded and their economies had greatly improved. It was considered that this might be due to their system of taxation.

We collected all the relevant statistics from economic sources and began to debate the issues. One of the factors which appeared to be important was the ease of collection of purchase tax. At the time of our report the points of collection numbered about 65,000. No one was quite sure what the number of points of collection of VAT would be, but the number of assessments to Schedule D tax in respect of trading and professional profits at that time was over two million and this gave some indication of the increased burden of work and administration that would arise, together with the increased possibilities of fraud. However, we all felt that it would be sensible to go to Paris and discuss the matter with the authorities there. In the course of the visit we met, among others, the acknowledged father of value added tax in France.

In France they advised us against VAT and explained that the main reason they had introduced it was to enable them to collect tax more readily from the French population. They went on to say that in their view the purchase tax we had in force was an excellent form of taxation and much superior to VAT. Finally they said that if only they had the British taxation system in France they felt that it would be a great stimulus to the French economy.

Our visit to Paris made a considerable impression on us all. As a result we said that we could find no valid reason for the introducton of a value added tax in substitution for the purchase tax. Also, that the balance of advantages fell positively against the substitution of a value added tax for the profits tax. These recommendations were adopted but, as is the way of things in politics, there is little stability in our financial policies. Value added tax was introduced in 1973 as a result of our joining the Common Market earlier in that year and it was also used as a means of replacing the revenue lost by the abolition of the Selective Employment Tax.

The CBI

In 1963 Sir Sam Brown, the senior partner of Linklaters & Paines, a leading firm of solicitors in London, and I were appointed as commissioners to undertake jointly the task of proposing a constitution of a National Industrial Organisation which would embrace the National Association of British Manufacturers (NABM), the Federation of British Industries (FBI) and the British Employers' Confederation (BEC).

Unfortunately, soon after we started work Sam Brown was taken seriously ill and, although he signed the report as indicating agreement with it, he took no part in the enquiry and I continued the task alone. Sam Brown died not long afterwards; we had been great friends for many years and I valued his advice in my business life and would have been glad to have worked with him on the enquiry.

The possibility of combining the three organisations had been examined on previous occasions but had come to nothing. There was a growing feeling, however, that the existence of the three bodies resulted in overlapping and sometimes divergent policies. It was considered that a single organisation was needed which could speak with authority for the country's productive industry in all its aspects and that it would provide a counterpoise to the growing influence of the trade union movement.

I found that, as the work developed, my main responsibility was one of persuasion. The NABM and the BEC were nervous of being swamped by the FBI which was relatively stronger. The FBI was nervous that its main objectives might be changed by the absorption of the other two.

In the course of this work I called upon George Woodcock, then general secretary of the TUC, to seek his views and to get any general advice which he could offer. He was most helpful and told me that he supported the proposal to bring about a single organisation. I asked him about the trade union organisation and whether there were not far too many separate trade unions (the number at that time was about 170). He said that, in his view, there were too many and that it hampered the administration of the trade union movement. I asked him why they were not reduced in number, and he said that it was not possible. There were a number of people in each of the separate unions who were dressed in a little brief authority and they were jealous of their rights and their position; he felt that they would be unwilling to merge into a larger body when they might get swamped or might lose the prestige and standing which they held in their own unions. In this respect he was too pessimistic because, by the pressure of events, the number has been greatly reduced; it is now only 88.

In due course, after consulting a large number of people in industry and in Whitehall, who were able to make useful contributions, and a great deal of dialogue with the three organisations, a structure with adequate safeguards was formulated which commanded the support of all three organisations. Acceptance of the report was therefore assured before publication. On issue it met with general acceptance by the public and after a period of negotiation on detail the Confederation of British Industry (CBI) came into being. The constitution recommended was that of a Royal Charter and for this purpose the existing Charter of the FBI was adapted appropriately.

I wrote a foreword to the report which is reproduced below and it represents fairly the views of a number of influential people at that time; it certainly encompassed my own convictions.

In the course of our enquiries we had discussions with a large number of people; men of wide knowledge who were experienced in almost all phases of industrial activity. We were impressed with the unanimity of their views which we also share. Almost without exception they welcomed the intention to set up a national organisation of this character and emphasised the leadership it could provide. They pointed out the need for an organisation which could speak with an authoritative voice for the productive industry of the country in all its aspects. They stressed the importance of a body which would represent to Government and to international organisations the views of British industry as a whole and to advise Government, when called upon to do so, on industrial problems. Greater opportunities were seen to be available for giving service to members, both large and small, on industrial problems at home and in export markets. Last, but not least, it was thought that the new organisation could provide a means of stimulating modern methods of management; of examining new techniques; and of exporting in greater depth than hitherto the problems of productivity and labour relations. Many subsidiary advantages were seen as likely to follow in the train of these basic functions of the new organisation.

Proposals to integrate the three existing organisations have been examined on previous occasions. In the light of the considerable body of evidence which has been put before us in recent months it is clear that a new approach to the formation of a national industrial organisation, on the lines proposed in our report, would be welcomed by a large number of those engaged in the management and direction of the productive industry of the country. Delay in arriving at a decision can, in our opinion, only be harmful.

8

Special Assignments 1964–74

Rolls Razor Ltd – The Bloom Case

In July 1964 the President of the Board of Trade, Edward Heath, appointed me as an inspector, jointly with Morris Finer QC, to investigate the affairs of Rolls Razor Ltd under the then provisions of Section 165 of the Companies Act 1948. The chairman of the company was John Bloom, and the company's main purpose was the production and sale of domestic washing machines at competitive prices.

The crisis in the company's affairs followed quickly after a programme about it which appeared on BBC television. Morris Finer and I thought that our first task was to see this and we went down to the BBC to watch a replay. After it was over we asked to talk to the person who was responsible for preparing the programme. My recollection is that he was 26 years old (though he may have been a year or two more) and he had no experience of working in industry. We asked him what had made the BBC put on this programme which appeared to have caused the collapse of the company. He said, 'I came to the conclusion that it was time . . .' but then stopped and began again. He said in effect that the BBC had come to the conclusion that a presentation on a company which was much in the public eye would be of pubic interest.

Morris Finer and I were both disturbed by this. It seemed to us dangerous that a young man with no understanding of industry could be put in a position to initiate and present a programme which could destroy a company employing a large number of people. We were told that Bloom had agreed to the presentation but Bloom later told us that he had not realised how much it would damage his business. It is also fair to say that our subsequent enquiries showed that the company would have collapsed anyhow in due course, unless vigorous steps had been taken in the meanwhile to reorganise its structure and finances. The young man said that before it was finally transmitted his programme had been carefully vetted by experienced lawyers to consider whether or not the programme was defamatory.

Morris Finer and I then attended in the board room of the company's offices to discuss matters with the directors. During the morning a bottle of orange squash was brought in on a battered tin tray and we were invited to have a drink out of some very thick glasses. We felt that this was an agreeable gesture by unsophisticated directors who wished to cooperate but did not know how to set about it. The initial view that Morris Finer and I formed, that the directors were inexperienced and largely victims of circumstance, proved to be wrong. One morning we met and found that we had both changed our minds virtually overnight. We felt that the business was rotten through and through and the more we looked into it the worse it became. The management was weak and inefficient, the company was under-capitalised, the accounts were unreliable, some of the stock valuations were suspect, and production problems had developed with the machinery and equipment incorporated in the washing machines which resulted in rejects and claims by dissatisfied customers which were continually increasing. The report was issued in November 1965, sixteen months later. In the course of time, after the police had made independent enquiries, arrests were made and some of the directors were later indicted for fraud for their part in the conduct of the company's affairs. The Board of Trade decided not to publish the report Morris Finer and I had made as it was considered that it might prevent a fair trial. In 1969, five years after the inspectors were appointed, the case against John Bloom was brought to trial. As a result of plea bargaining he pleaded guilty to certain charges and was fined £30,000. The leader of the Crown prosecution team explained to me the difficulty of presenting a complicated case to a jury some years after the event. The case was stale and there was also the problem, by that time, of finding witnesses who could provide reliable oral evidence. Accordingly, he was satisfied that the arrangement was the only possible course open. I see no objection to plea bargaining under certain defined conditions and I believe that, under proper safeguards, the practice could usefully be extended, thereby saving an enormous amount of time and expense. But the Bloom case nevertheless caused some disquiet among members of the legal fraternity who were familiar with all the circumstances.

Working with Morris Finer was an agreeable experience. He had a razor sharp mind and a keen sense of humour. He was later appointed a High Court Judge, but unhappily died in 1974 before the strength of his intellect and his character could make itself felt on the Bench. The problem of presenting complex fraud cases to the jury is one which came prominently into my life a few years later when I sat as a member of the Roskill Committee and when I was engaged on the Carrian case.

The Steel Industry

In March 1966 I was appointed by the British Iron and Steel Federation as chairman of a committee 'to consider all aspects of iron and steel industry rationalisation and coordinated development, to examine the impact of possible proposals on the industry's future competitiveness and its ability to meet the particular needs of the British economy and to report'. The other members of the committee were E T Judge, Sir Duncan Oppenheim, A J Peach, Sir Julian Pode and Sir Peter Runge. The purpose of this enquiry was well judged but it was far too late. The steel industry had been nationalised by the Labour government in 1949 and denationalised by the Conservative government in 1961. The denationalisation was accompanied by threats from the Labour opposition, when they returned to power, to renationalise the industry – an event which took place in 1967.

The Labour party's policy of nationalising the country's major industries while beneficial and imperative in some cases, such as the coal industry, was disrupting and damaging in others. In the years during which the steel industry was treated like an industrial shuttlecock the effect was disastrous. Industries which are threatened with nationalisation tend to distribute as much as possible to the shareholders while the going is good and to postpone large-scale and long-term reorganisation schemes. Each company chooses what is best for itself and the overall future of the industry and its competitiveness in world markets is forgotten. So it was in the steel industry. Before the second nationalisation took place in 1967 the British Iron and Steel Federation realised the damage which was being done to the industry and our committee was therefore set up. Its purpose was to plan the big changes which were needed if the steel industry under private ownership was to remain competitive in world markets. Rationalisation schemes and expenditure on capital assets involving very large sums of money were necessary; mergers and amalgamations were inevitable.

If the committee had been appointed some three years earlier, and action had been taken to implement its recommendations, it is possible that the second nationalisation might not have taken place. By 1966 the industry could have shown that it was adapting itself to the needs of the day and there would have been no grounds, except political dogma, for subjecting it yet again to the unsettlement of nationalisation. While the committee's work was at mid-stage, the Labour government confirmed its intention to nationalise yet again the greater part of the steel industry and the relevant Bill was introduced just as the committee was concluding its task.

The first report by the committee was published in July 1966. It made, in the short period of four months, a comprehensive review of the state of the steel industry and indicated, but did not at that time specify in detail, that major schemes of rationalisation and regrouping were necessary. The first report was followed by a second report which was finished in February 1967. There was doubt whether the second report was worth completing in view of the government's determination to nationalise. However, it was completed because it was felt that it might be helpful to indicate the regrouping which, in the committee's view, was needed in any event and to consider how far it could be expected to have been achieved by the mid-1970s if it had been put into force.

The second report was not, however, published by the Iron and Steel Federation and it has never seen the light of day. It was felt that the disclosure of the groupings would have a dramatic effect on the share price of some of the steel companies and this would be damaging at a time when the compensation terms under the nationalisation scheme were being settled. Also, the proposals for nationalisation had by that time advanced so far that the recommendations in the second report were likely to be of little practical value.

In due course the steel industry was nationalised for the second time in 1967. It had a difficult birth and a chequered career in its early childhood. This is not surprising because the British Steel Corporation, under its first chairman, Lord Melchett, had not only to overcome the formidable problems of integrating large and diverse iron and steel companies but it had to begin the huge task of reorganisation which the committee's two reports had indicated as necessary if the steel industry was to be efficient and capable of competing in world markets.

The Conservative government privatised the British steel industry again in 1988. One is left to wonder whether, and when, the steel industry will be nationalised for the third time.

The National Trust

In 1967 I was appointed chairman of an advisory committee to review the management, organisation and responsibilities of the National Trust. The other members were Pat Gibson (later Lord Gibson), who subsequently himself became chairman of the National Trust, L J Clark and Sir William Hayter KCMG. Of all the tasks I have undertaken I think the results of this committee's work have given me the greatest satisfaction.

The National Trust, which was started in 1894, was a great concept. Many people believe that its assets belong to the government, which is in a position to deal with them as it wishes. This is not so. It is a charity and is independent of government supervision and control except insofar as its activities are subject, like those of other charities, to the scrutiny of the Charity Commissioners.

At the time of our appointment the trust was subject to the National Trust Act of 1907 and of 1937. The former provided that it should be established for the purposes of promoting the permanent preservation, for the benefit of the nation, of lands and tenements (including buildings) of beauty or historic interest and as regards lands, for the preservation (as far as practicable) of their natural aspect, features and animal and plant life. Any person was entitled to become a member of the National Trust on payment of the appropriate subscription.

In the early years the Trust grew slowly but in the years prior to the committee's appointment, and especially after the Second World War, it had been enlarged a great deal. One of the reasons was the diminution in assets and income of many of the former landowning families because of death duties and high taxation. They were glad to make over their properties to the Trust and it was often provided that those then in ownership could continue to live there during their lifetime. This rapid growth in assets, some of which were not adequately endowed, placed great burdens on the

Trust's finances. The quality of people who served the Trust was high but the structure and administration were not well suited to its growing responsibilities and it needed overhaul to enable it to manage its affairs and plan properly for the future.

The committee examined every aspect of the Trust's affairs and made about sixty recommendations, the bulk of which were accepted after the Council of the Trust had examined each in detail.

The following were the major recommendations which were made:

- There should be greater decentralisation to regional committees which should in future be organised on a uniform basis.
- The Trust should not accept properties in future unless they were fully endowed and could, with assurance, be made self-supporting.
- Greater access should be given to properties which in the past had been inadequate. This would also help to raise the Trust's revenue.
- In the ensuing fifteen years a target should be set to raise the ordinary membership to 500,000.
- An improved system of budgetary control should be introduced throughout the organisation.
- There should be an increase in the amenities provided at the Trust's properties.
- A more vigorous and lively attention to public relations should be adopted in the future.

In the years since the report was published the Trust has continued to grow and it is now an organisation of great size which owns and administers a large number of valuable properties and lands. Finance is always a problem for a charity and the Trust's future depends upon the continued support of the public. The following is a comparison of the position in 1967 when we made our report and the situation twenty years later.

	1967	1987
Gross income	£301,887	£87,083,000
Gross assets other than properties and chattels held for preservation	£10,151,633	£171,090,000
Total membership	152,000	1,545,913
Number of visitors to properties open at a charge	2,569,705	8,519,731
Mileage of coast protected	250	500
Areas of land owned	351,572 acres	548,000 acres

An irritating problem which had plagued the Trust about that time was a member of the public who was convinced that the Trust employed some homosexuals on its staff and he caused much distress and irritation by making innuendoes to that effect in various places. He eventually came to give evidence to the committee. At the end of a long and tiresome meeting I said, spontaneously and with conviction, that I was sorry I could not help him because I had never been able to detect a homosexual from a heterosexual. There was nothing more to be said on the subject and his campaign petered out soon afterwards.

The Horse Racing Industry

Also in 1967 I was appointed by the Stewards of the Jockey Club and the Stewards of the National Hunt Committee as chairman of a committee to enquire into the position of the horse racing industry in the United Kingdom. The terms of reference were long and detailed. The simple facts were that the racing industry was going through a bad patch. The prize money was quite inadequate to justify the expenditure which race horse owners had to incur if they were to keep horses in training. This affected the whole industry including breeders, trainers, jockeys and the racecourses. There was particular anxiety that the quality of the livestock bred in this country would deteriorate and that, as a result, racing itself would eventually come to an end.

Horse racing is like every other sport. Those who are interested in it are dedicated followers, not only on the racecourse itself but in the excitements of betting. Those who are not interested in it find it dull and boring. The sport has a very long history in Britain. Complete and detailed records of race meetings in Great Britain were started early in the eighteenth century, but horse races are known to have been held in the third century and the Chester races first took place in 1540.

In those early years, racing was solely a sport in which owners raced their horses against each other for private amusement. At that time the men who indulged in it had the means and leisure to do so. In the intervening years social change and the increasing burdens of taxation have brought radical alterations. It is no longer a pastime for the wealthy. Racing remains a sport, but it is also an industry which depends on the support of the public for its survival and it provides occupation and employment for over 150,000 people. People who are interested in the breeding, training and racing of horses will still be glad to spend part of their resources, according to their means, to engage in the sport, but the number who can afford under present taxation conditions to set aside more than a modest sum is small and is diminishing annually. In short, if racing is to survive it must continue to excite the interest of the public and at the same time provide adequate remuneration or rewards for those who are engaged in it.

The other members of my committee were the Marquess of Abergavenny, Sir Rex Cohen KBE and Major W D Gibson, who had all taken a keen interest in racing all their lives. I was appointed because it was considered desirable to appoint someone who was independent. On that ground, no better choice could have been made. I hardly knew one end of a horse from another and I had no knowledge of the intricacies of the racing world. We set about our task by making enquiries in other countries. Personal visits were paid by a member, or by the secretary, of the committee to Australia, Canada, France, Ireland, New Zealand, South

Africa and the USA. A representative of the committee visited West Malaysia and Singapore. In addition, of course, we took oral and written evidence from a large number of organisations and members of the public. While the enquiry was in progress I was asked to attend upon the Queen to indicate the range of our enquiries and to answer some points on which she wished to make enquiry. When the report was published we asked her to accept from the committee a copy of the report bound in leather. It is not unusual for reports by committees to be referred to afterwards, for convenience, by the name of the chairman. On publication, the racing industry work was usually referred to as the Benson Report, and I notice that this also happened with the reports on the National Trust and the Royal Commission on Legal Services.

As is usual in all such reports we made a survey of the whole subject supported by a large volume of statistics. We concluded by making seventy-five recommendations but the main thrust of the report was based on one sentence, which said: 'The whole future of the racing industry is dependent on fixing an adequate level of prize money.' Much of the report was directed at how this could best be achieved.

When published the report received a good deal of publicity in the racing world and it stimulated discussion and activity throughout the industry. As the years have gone by, the industry has increased and prospered. The prize money in the majority of races has greatly improved and is presently high enough to encourage the breeding and training of horses. British bloodstock has maintained its reputation and can hold its own with France, the USA and other countries which are interested in the sport.

As a result of this work, I was elected a member of the Jockey Club. I was later appointed a Steward of Goodwood Racecourse but after a few years I resigned because I came to the conclusion that I was not skilled enough, despite attending a course which was run by the Jockey Club for amateur Stewards. I took part in any Stewards' enquiry at meetings I attended at Goodwood but I felt that the decisions needed a more expert and intimate knowledge than mine. The only decision I ever had to make on my own occurred because I happened to arrive early on the course one morning. A bird had built a nest and was sitting on eggs in the stable which was used by the veterinary officers for inspecting horses which were selected at random by the Stewards for tests for doping. There were three courses open – to destroy the nest; or to leave the stable empty; or to continue to use the stable, which might upset the bird and possibly the horse. I decided that the stable should be closed and that the bird (and maybe the horse) should be left in peace.

The Ministry of Defence

In 1969 Denis Healey, who was Minister for Defence, set up a committee to consider the structure and organisation of the Department under the chairmanship of the Permanent Secretary, Sir James Dunnett. I was one of two people from outside the Department appointed to the committee. We saw Denis Healey from time to time and I was impressed by the clarity of his objectives and his detailed grasp of the problems which we were asked to enquire into. Our paths have crossed many times since then in one way or another and I have always enjoyed our meetings, although I have a different outlook on some political issues. The report was for internal use only and some of the information had the classification of 'secret' so I had to be cleared especially to receive the relevant documents. I was not provided with a copy of the report for retention after the work was concluded and there is little upon which it is appropriate for me to comment. We held a great many meetings and covered a wide range of subjects.

Rolls-Royce

Early in 1970 the financial stability of Rolls-Royce Ltd became suspect. Some time previously the company had designed and secured substantial orders from America for a new aero engine known as the RB211 which was to be fitted in the American Lockheed Tristar aircraft. This received great publicity and was hailed as a major engineering triumph for a British company. Producing a new aero engine and putting it into production is a great industrial hazard. The design and development costs are enormous and it is difficult to estimate with any degree of accuracy what the final cost will be, years later, when engines finally begin to come off the production line. Unforeseen delays invariably occur and the cost of the learning curve, that is to say, the training of staff in the new production techniques, is often underestimated. Indeed, the technical success of the engine itself is not assured until it has been tested under normal working conditions for some time.

All these problems had assailed, or were assailing, Rolls-Royce to a greater or lesser degree. It became obvious that the company was running out of money and that the contract, when completed, would inflict heavy losses on the company. If Rolls-Royce failed, the longer-term consequences of the damage to British prestige in America would be grave and the effect on Lockheed would be disastrous. When the first rumbles of trouble were heard my firm was appointed by the government to make an investigation and report and I was responsible for this task.

The investigation had not proceeded very far when it was overtaken by events. It was plain that the company would not be able to continue in its present form unless there was a reorganisation and an immediate and massive injection of cash. I reported orally to this effect to the Permanent Secretary at the Ministry of Aviation Supply, Sir Ronald Melville. He felt that the matter was of such national importance that the Prime Minister should be informed without delay. We attended at Downing Street that evening at about 9 pm and I explained the situation as I saw it to Edward Heath.

I also asked the government's permission to inform the Governor of the Bank of England, Leslie O'Brien (later Lord O'Brien of Lothbury). I was fearful that news of a possible crash of this magnitude would cause disruption in the financial markets because the large liabilities of the company which would not be paid might jeopardise the survival of many of Rolls-Royce's suppliers. He was, I think, grateful for having been alerted to what might happen so that he could take appropriate action. His patience must, however, have been stretched to the limit as my nose bled copiously during the meeting and at the lunch he provided afterwards.

In due course the critical position of the company, and the necessity for a decision as to what course to adopt, reached Cabinet level. I waited in the anteroom in Downing Street with the Permanent Secretary in case clarification was needed on any point and I was duly called into the meeting. This was unusual as it is not customary for outsiders to attend a Cabinet meeting; the Permanent Secretary, much to his chagrin, was not allowed to accompany me. The Prime Minister was in the chair. On his right was the secretary of the Cabinet and I was placed next to him. A woman was on my right who I thought was a secretary taking the minutes.

There were three courses open:

1. To let the company collapse. This would have been consistent with the government's policy at that time of non-intervention in industrial problems but, as already explained, the consequences would have been grave.

2. For the government to announce that it would nationalise the company and provide whatever money was required to meet its existing liabilities and its outstanding committees to complete the RB211 contract.

3. For the company to appoint a receiver. This would enable great economies to be effected at once. It gave the receiver the opportunity of completing the contract without being weighed down by existing liabilities and the burdens of the past losses. Some money for completing the RB211 contract would still be required from the government but it would be restricted in amount and capable of close control.

I believed that the third course was the only sensible one to follow. I was questioned by members of the Cabinet on all these issues for a considerable time. Cross-examination at best is a trying experience, but when unconnected questions (not always clearly expressed) are thrown at one from all round the room it becomes a very testing exercise. From time to time the woman on my right suggested points, *sotto voce*, but this added to my difficulties because it meant that I was trying to listen to two people at the same time: I turned round with a sharp expression of impatience to quieten the interruption. After the meeting was over I stayed behind to deal with some cables which had to be despatched to America and the person on my right was introduced to me as the Secretary of State for Education, Mrs Thatcher.

In due course the Cabinet adopted the third course and a receiver was appointed who conducted the company's affairs with skill and competence. The aero engine contract was completed and the engine proved a success in practice. Both the aero engine and the motor car sections of the business survived and prospered; they are in existence today, although they are now in separate companies with different shareholders.

Ten years later I was again in the Cabinet Room for a meeting of a small number of people to discuss an industrial problem. The Prime Minister, Mrs Thatcher, was in the chair. Before the meeting began she asked me with good humour whether I remembered the last occasion I was there and said, 'You sat there and I sat next to you.' We both remembered what had happened ten years before, and I hope I blushed with embarrassment.

Girobank

In 1968 Girobank was set up under the initiative of the Labour government then in power. At that time Telecom and the Post Office were under single ownership and Girobank was a subsidiary undertaking, working in close contact (as it does now) with the 20,000 branches of the Post

Office. The bank had a slow and uneasy start and there were defects in the early management. It made losses in its early years. When the Conservative government came into office in 1970 one of the proposals it had under consideration was the abolition of the bank.

I was asked to make a report on this proposal. It was hoped by some who were helping to shape Conservative policy that I would recommend that Girobank should be closed down. In fact my report arrived at the opposite conclusion. After I had had an opportunity of studying the situation in detail, I came to the conclusion that it should be kept in being and that every opportunity should be taken by the government to make it a success.

It was a new form of money transmission system and was justified on its merits. It provided competition for the existing banks and would be helpful to citizens at the lower end of the social spectrum. The giro system works well on the continent of Europe and is widely used there. The defects in management and the early losses are typical of what often happens when a new, large enterprise, starts from scratch. I felt that the defects in management could be corrected and once the business transacted reached a certain volume, the losses would turn into profits.

The report was not welcomed in Conservative quarters but in the event the recommendations were accepted and Girobank remained in existence. Twenty years after it began the bank was making profits, before tax, of over £20 million, and it then claimed that it was the sixth largest bank in the United Kingdom though it is, of course, a long way behind the four major clearing banks in size. In 1988 the Conservative government decided to privatise Girobank and to offer it for sale by auction. The price tag put on it was in the region of £100-£200 million.

9.

The Bank of England 1975-83

I retired from Coopers & Lybrand on 31 March 1975 at 65, which was the age then specified in our partnership agreement. It has since been reduced, as is the case in a large number of pension arrangmeents in the City and in industry. I was wondering how I should fill my time when Gordon Richardson, the Governor of the Bank, asked me to call on him. I had known the Governor for many years when he was chairman of the merchant bank, Schroders Ltd, who were clients of the firm. In 1962 I had also sat on the VAT committee, of which he was chairman. He invited me to join the Bank as an adviser to the Governor and I found myself installed in the 'parlours' (as the rooms adjacent to the Governor's are called) before the end of April 1975.

I was not given any specific terms of reference when I began but was available on any problem of finance affecting industry and commerce which was where my main previous experience lay. I think also that the Governor was anxious, among other things, for the Bank to study its links with industry and commerce, a subject on which he was naturally interested as a former merchant banker. The Bank had an efficient intelligence system but it was not directly concerned with the provision of finance for, or the quality of the management in, industry. In the 1930s after the crippling recession of 1929-31 the Bank was interested in the resuscitation of industry but during and after the Second World War this aspect of its work diminished.

I doubt if it is generaly realised how closely the Bank keeps in touch with industry. Even before I joined it was the practice for an executive director on the Court of the Bank, or a senior member of the top management to visit the provinces accompanied by one or two members of less senior staff. They would visit a different works in the morning and in the afternoon on two consecutive days. In the evenings (and sometimes at lunch) the chairmen, managing directors, or finance directors of companies in the neighbourhood would be invited to dinner (or lunch). The senior member of the Bank's team would give a survey of the economic scene after which a general discussion followed. These were interesting and important. They disclosed both the local and general problems which were affecting industry; the effect of government measures; the damaging or favourable effects on exports at the ruling rate of exchange; and other matters. A careful record of all these visits was made and circulated within the Bank and in government departments. By these means the Bank had a remarkable grasp of what was happening in industry at the grass roots. The Bank has eight offices in the provinces, each of which is headed by a full-time employee of the Bank who is known as an 'agent'. The agents are punctilious about keeping the Bank in London informed about anything of importance taking place in their areas. They were also of great assistance in arranging these visits and keeping the visiting team in touch with local affairs. I think a particular benefit was the number of occasions on which directors of different businesses met each other for the first time at dinner parties given by the Bank, although for years they had lived and worked in the same city.

Primarily the Bank of England is the bankers' bank and, of course, it acts as adviser to the government on a large number of financial and economic matters. The Governor is the link between the City and the government and his opposite number is the Chancellor of the Exchequer. In times of financial crisis his advice and opinions can, in practice, be decisive even to the point of overriding or varying the government's political wishes. At the time I joined the Governor himself was careful to make it clear that he regarded his position as head of the City as one of his specific responsibilities, and this was acknowledged by all those who carried on business within the square mile. He is, of course, in regular touch with the banking community and he used to have, and no doubt still has, meetings with the heads of other institutions in the City when the need arose. Gordon Richardson was keenly interested in every aspect of city life. He expected to be kept informed of any important event or development and if he was not so informed, he took steps to find out. This was important because the Bank's influence can be decisive. An indication of the Governor's disapproval would often prevent a course of action or, if approval is given, ensure its success.

In the ordinary course of events I doubt whether there would have been enough work in the Bank to occupy me fully but about that time the country was entering into a period of industrial recession, high inflation and rising unemployment. Companies were beginning to get into financial difficulty. The Bank's involvement began in a modest way, but escalated as the recession deepened. Either through his own initiative, or because he was informed as head of the City, the Governor began to be aware that some of our industrial companies were getting into serious financial difficulty. Companies are normally, and properly, reticent about discussing their affairs with anybody except their professional advisers and their bankers. When approached, however, they were willing to confide in the Bank for two reasons. First, the Bank was trusted implicitly. Second, they knew that the Bank's approach would be impartial, independent and confidential. No fee was ever expected or demanded and they were glad to have any help which was available. In some such cases it soon became evident that the problems were deep-seated. A typical example would be a large industrial company or group which had taken out lines of credit with a number of different bankers but there was no lead banker in the group who knew the whole picture. As soon as crisis loomed, some of the smaller banks, who had been intent on securing business at cut rates, called their loans which merely precipitated or aggravated the crisis. The number of banks varied; it could be no more than two or three but often it was as high as twenty or more.

The solution was for the Bank, using its authority and prestige, to call the participating banks together and, if there was no lead banker, to arrange for one of the major lenders to assume that position. At this, or later, meetings the position of all the various banks was exposed and a solution was propounded by the Bank with help from the lead banker or from a merchant bank appointed for that purpose. Intense negotiations followed. Various steps had to be taken depending on the circumstances but in no case, during my term of eight years, was money ever put up by the Bank itself. Banks who wished to call their loans were persuaded not to do so; sometimes new money had to be provided for survival and one or all of the banks was persuaded to provide it, with or without some special arrangements as to security or priority of repayment. Sometimes the help of a major industrial shareholder was sought who undertook to provide new money for an appropriate term. The company's management often had to be changed either by agreement or as a condition of continued support by the banks and the institutional shareholders. The search for better management, when needed, was a constant headache and we had a difficult task to find, at short notice, people who were able and willing to take on rescue operations of one sort or another. Sometimes the need for action was urgent so that wages could be paid at the end of the week and pressing creditors paid off; meetings often took place late into the night.

If the need rose, the Bank did not hesitate to exercise the full weight of its authority and influence. I remember one occasion when two overseas banks with branches in London had refused to agree to a scheme which had been approved by all the other banks. A decision was urgent. The two banks were called into the Bank about 8 o'clock that evening for further talks and put into separate rooms. The first of the two remained obdurate and they were then asked for the telephone number of the chairman of the bank at its headquarters overseas. There was an ominous pause and the local representatives said that they were reluctant to bother the chairman with this problem and they would like a few minutes to consider the matter further. We moved into the other room and the same treatment was meted out to the other recalcitrant banker. In the end agreement was given by both by 9 o'clock without recourse to the overseas telephone.

The Bank naturally became sensitive to the need to detect trouble in good time. The Bank's agents in the provinces had a great many contacts with industry in their areas and they were diligent in informing Threadneedle Street if trouble was suspected. The Bank also instituted a practice of surveying the published accounts of all the quoted industrial companies with an annual turnover of over £20 million. The annual reports were studied with care and the financial statements were tested by a number of standard ratios over a four-year period, such as return on capital employed, debt equity ratios, ratio of stocks and debtors to turnover, and other indicators, including adjustment of the figures to current as opposed to historical costs. It soon became apparent which companies were drifting into trouble and steps were taken to get in touch with them or with their bankers for discussions. It was surprising how often large and well-known companies and their bankers had not realised that trouble lay ahead of them. One of the basic reasons was that they had not realised the damaging effects of rampant inflation. An industrial company, employing heavy and costly machinery and equipment, would show what appeared to be a good return on capital employed based on historical costs but, when translated into current costs, the company was in fact making losses.

In the early days of the recession the banks were not well organised to deal with these crises among their major clients. In due course they set up special units to cope with problem cases to which some of their best managers were appointed. This helped to ease the strain put on the Bank of England. The banks are now much quicker to spot signs of trouble but when the Bank first started these rescue operations it often had to alert a sceptical London banker to the dangers which were facing one or other of his client companies.

I felt very strongly about the eroding effects of inflation and made a point of it in my maiden speech in the House of Lords on 11 March 1981. The passage quoted below comes from that speech:

I wish to speak on a single narrow sector of this huge subject – financial management. It has been my lot in life to examine many businesses both large and small. Those who are not competitive, who have failed, or have been unsuccessful and unprofitable, have one common fault running through them all – an inability to realise quickly enough the damaging effects of inflation and weak financial policies. The signs are unmistakable: an inadequate return on capital employed, excessive borrowing, inadequate retentions, dividends when expressed in real terms paid out of capital, wrong pricing policies, bad estimating, loose control of stock and debtors and an inability to plan forward, particularly the cash flow, which results in an erratic investment programme.

Not all but many of those would have been avoided if it had been realised early enough that accounts prepared on the historical cost convention, both annual and management accounts, are misleading, and need to be adjusted to real terms to reflect the effects of inflation. Particularly is this the case of fixed assets and stock. Unhappily there are many people in this country who have not yet been able to adjust themselves to this modern form of accounting. They decry, deride and denigrate it and that is a grievous impediment to industrial progress.

I have recently been reading the life of Lord Lister. His great discoveries on antiseptic surgery were met with opposition, ridicule and apathy. Indeed when his opponents noticed that the incisions they made in their patients' bodies were beginning to suppurate they expressed great satisfaction and referred to it by the disagreeable name of 'laudable pus'. The analogy is complete. Until we in this country learn that management and annual accounts prepared on the historical cost convention are no better than laudable pus, so long will a large number of our businesses move remorselessly and deservedly to the mortuary.

Another event took place while I was at the Bank which, I believe, had important long-term effects. One Friday afternoon a person whom I did not know came to see me. He said he knew that the Governor wished to be kept informed about important events in the City and he wished to acquaint me with the following facts.

He said the company of which he was a director had discovered a massive fraud following a takeover they had made of another company. The confrontation was to take place at 9 am on Monday. He thought that the news would leak and because of the size and importance of the problem he wished the Governor of the Bank to be informed. I asked my informant whether I could see the Department of Trade and Industry and was given permission. I told the Governor what had happened and then went to the Department of Trade and Industry and urged them to use whatever powers were available to protect the papers and documents of the company which I thought would otherwise be destroyed. Finally I went to the offices of the company's solicitors where I again met my informant and the company's auditors. I suggested to them that the company should call in the help of the auditors to place a member of the audit staff in front of every safe and cabinet in the company's offices at 8.45 on Monday to protect their records. As events turned out, none of the people whom I had alerted to the risks of the situation were able to, or did, take any action.

On the Tuesday morning at 7.30 am my informant telephoned me at home in London. He was in some distress. He said that on Monday afternoon a van had left the company's offices full of papers; it had been driven into the country. He had watched a bonfire all night but could not get close because of guard dogs. He asked me what he should do? My inclination was to say that as, contrary to most specific advice, he had left the stable door open, there was nothing he could do except kick himself. I advised him to get in touch with the police at once.

I made a detailed written report of these events to the
Governor. About that time there was growing anxiety in the
City and elsewhere about the increase in commercial fraud
cases and the apparent inability to bring fraudsters to book.
Indeed there was evidence that some fraudsters were using
London as a base in preference to other capital cities
because our lax procedures facilitated their operations. The
events desribed above reached the appropriate government
department in due course and this led to a wide-ranging
departmental enquiry as to the steps which could be taken
to improve procedures. The alarm about the incidence of
fraud continued to grow, however, and this ultimately led to
the setting up in 1984 of the Roskill Committee, of which I
became a member. It is referred to in Chapter 12.

There were some other matters with which I was
concerned during my service at the Bank. My experience in
dealing with companies in difficulty led me to note in many
cases the absence of any non-executive directors or, if they
existed, with the poor quality of those in post. Non-
executive directors should be able to stand back and look at
the company's overall performance and to initiate better
policies and better executive management when the
company's affairs begin to flag. I noticed that they did not
take steps to see that they were presented at regular intervals
with the essential factors on which the business depended,
such as the long- and short-term plans, performance
indicators, financial information including profits and
losses and cash flow, and reports on the position and
difficulties in different phases of the business. Even in those
cases where they received this information, they took no
effective steps to get to grips with the situation. Good non-
executive directors are not easy to find and, only too often,
they are 'yes' men who are appointed by the chairman to
support his own position. There are still many guinea pigs
on the market who want the security of a directorship on a
good board, but are not willing to face their special and
particular responsibilities. In this country we need to breed
a good strain of non-executive directors but the gestation

period, and the time needed for schooling, are considerable.

The idea was born therefore of setting up an organisation, subsequently called 'Proned', which would undertake to provide the names of people, carefully selected for the purpose, who might be suitable for appointment as non-executive directors for a particular company which needed them. Efforts were made at the same time in speeches and articles to alert companies and their institutional shareholders to ensure that an adequate number of competent non-executives were appointed to the board.

In due course Proned came into existence. It was financed by contributions from the Bank, the clearing bankers, the British Institute of Management, the CBI, the Stock Exchange and other City institutions. Initially no charge was made for this service, but latterly I understand modest fees were payable. The first chairman of Proned was Sir Maurice Laing who had been a member of the Court of the Bank for many years. Proned also published a booklet on the role of the non-executive director which should be made compulsory reading for every company director executive or non-executive.

Another venture was the formation of Equity Capital for Industry (ECI). At the time I joined the Bank, the growing recession and the mounting tide of inflation made it clear that there would be a shortage of equity capital for industry. The concept was that a company should be formed, the capital of which would be provided primarily by the institutions and pension funds who, with their collective strength, would be able to support medium-sized businesses with the equity capital some of them were clearly likely to need. The Bank, therefore, took the initiative of setting up a working party to consider the problem. ECI duly came into existence, but at the outset it was not popular. Some thought that it might take business away from the sources in the City which were normally responsible for providing finance. A condition was therefore attached to ECI's existence that it should only undertake business which could not be achieved through the usual market channels. I was opposed to this condition and still believe it was an absurd one to impose, but ECI would not otherwise have come into existence. A few years later the condition was abandoned and ECI now undertakes a considerable volume of business in providing equity capital at the small end of the market; it is earning good profits.

The problems of industry which were exposed to the Bank in those difficult years made it clear that a very large number of people who were concerned with industry – directors, accountants, lawyers, managers at the branches of the banks, and others – were unaware of the huge and divergent resources which were available for providing or helping to find capital for industry and commerce. These were the banks, the merchant banks, numerous financial institutions of one sort or another, and a wide range of government assistance schemes. In 1978, therefore, the Bank published *Money for Business* in conjunction with the City Communications Centre. It was a mine of useful information and many thousands of copies were either sold or distributed. The publication is updated from time to time and is still in issue. A sister volume, *Money for Exports*, was issued in 1979 but it was a one-off publication.

Shortly before I retired a small incident occurred which carried me back nearly fifty years. A man telephoned from somewhere in Oxfordshire in obvious distress. He said that he was running a small business which was successful and profitable but he needed more money for some modest re-equipment and working capital. He had tried every source and was on his beam-ends. His bankers were adamant that they would go no further and he was faced with liquidation in a fortnight. He said the Bank of England was the only source which he felt was left to him. I asked him how much he needed and he said £300,000. The similarity to the situation in which I found myself when I first entered the portals of the Bank in 1937 struck an emotional chord. I used the same language to him as had been used to me at that time. I said we could not ourselves put up money and we could not ask bankers to exceed what in their view was a sound banking decision, but if he would come and see me I would see if there was anything to be done. In due course, after enquiring into the business, we were able to find for him the resources he needed. I am told that the business is still flourishing, although it has since been taken over by another, larger organisation.

After serving the Bank for eight years I retired in 1983 at my own request on my seventy-fourth birthday. The Bank is an agreeable place in which to work. The accommodation is comfortable thanks to the foresight of Sir Herbert Baker when he rebuilt it in the late 1920s. The staff are friendly and helpful not only to colleagues but, in my experience, to anyone who seeks advice and assistance. There is another agreeable feature which makes it particularly interesting: one knows what is going on in the financial world and, because of the close association with Whitehall, what is taking place in financial and economic matters in the upper reaches of the government.

Bankers have always been attentive to the comfort and interests of their staff. As long ago as 1913, the clearing banks pressed for writers' cramp to be listed as a disease entitling the staff to workers' compensation. The Bank of England for its part has been an exemplary employer since it received its charter in 1694, but being a good employer does not warrant unseemly behaviour and some rules which held until comparatively recent times indicate that good discipline has always prevailed. Instant dismissal was the penalty if a member of staff got himself into circumstances of pecuniary embarrassment, was disordered with liquor, embraced the Roman Catholic faith, smoked cigars in the Bank, or refused to work on the Sabbath. Lenient treatment was accorded to moustaches and all that happened was that 'measures were resorted to of a painful character'. Women were, of course, physically segregated from the men and until clothes rationing in 1941 were required to wear long sleeves and white collars. The most considerate provision, however, was that any work requiring intelligence and education was to be given only to men. At the time I joined the Bank I think that some of these arrangements may have been modified but, during my tenure of office, I do not remember being in breach of any of them.

My remuneration when I joined the Bank, at my own request, was very modest and I later asked for it to be reduced by one-third. I worked hard but I felt that it was a retirement job and I was lucky to be there at all. When I left, the Bank generously said that my wife and I could make a visit anywhere in the world at their expense. We therefore went to Zambia to see the animals in their natural state in the Luangwa valley. Then on to South Africa to see other animals in the shape of my relations there. We came back via India, a country which I had never visited before, and completed the tour by calling in a Dubai to see some friends, and at Rome for cultural uplift. It lasted four weeks and gave us much pleasure.

The scene which the Governor views from the Bank is now changing because the machinery of the City has undergone notable alterations since the Big Bang in October 1986. Before that the different organisations operating in the square mile were specialists in their own particular fields, and stuck to their lasts like good shoemakers. They have now extended their activities so that they carry out each other's business. For example, stockbrokers used to act as agents in the sole interests of their clients, but they can now act both as principal and agent. Many stockbroking firms have been absorbed by merchant banks. The clearing banks have subsidiary companies which act as merchant banks and dealers in securities. Confidential information which comes into the possession of a concern from one of its clients can, if used, have a profound effect on other operations carried out on its own account. 'Chinese walls' are being erected to prevent sensitive information from being used improperly, but this is a brittle structure and there is anxiety in the public mind that the walls are not always secure.

One result of this massive rearrangement of functions is that a number of young people have been placed in positions of great responsibility, and paid grossly extravagant salaries and other rewards, without the necessary training or experience. This should correct itself in time but in the meanwhile it is causing great irritation to those who are attempting to recruit talent for industry and other employment because the able young are being attracted to the City by these corrupting influences. In consequence of these and other similar changes, conflicts of interest and risks of insider dealing have multiplied, and trust, which was the hallmark of the City, has temporarily at least been impaired.

Another major innovation has been the formation of supervisory bodies for the purpose of so-called 'self-regulation', and to ensure that the conduct of financial transactions is carefully scrutinised. This is imposing on the City a heavy burden of overhead expenses and bureaucratic control, which will increase costs materially. It is too early to judge the effect of all this, but some of the older hands in the City, like myself, are uneasy, and feel that there will have to be many more changes to overcome the self-inflicted problems which have been created in the last few years.

10.

The Royal Commission on
Legal Services 1976-79

In 1976, I was asked to be chairman of a Royal Commission on Legal Services and the Governor was kind enough to allow me to undertake the task although my full-time commitment was, of course, to the Bank. When I went to Downing Street to accept the appointment, I said I would do so on condition that I could approve the secretary. This was not a capricious request because I knew that unless the secretary was of high quality my job would be impossible. I went on to the Lord Chancellor's department and after a long interview approved the proposed secretary, John Heritage, who, in due course, fulfilled the task with distinction. Later I saw the Lord Chancellor, Lord Elwyn-Jones, and urged him to try to ensure that the total number appointed to the Commission was not more than ten, a view with which he agreed; he said he would make representations to the Prime Minister to that effect. This was important. In a long and difficult enquiry a big membership is an encumbrance because meetings comprising a large number of people have to be kept formal in character and it is difficult to allow everybody to say all that they want in the time available. There is no opportunity for the cut and thrust of a round table discussion as is the case if membership is, say, eight (or at most) ten in number. A few weeks later the membership of the Commission was announced, fifteen in number, which was very irritating in view of my request to the Lord Chancellor.

I did not find the problems raised by the Commission terms of reference especially difficult. The burden was of a different nature. The number of Commissioners was uncomfortably large and the political bias of the members was diverse, and strongly evident. Far too often problems seemed to me to be approached on the basis of dogma rather than objectivity. It is extraordinary, however, how a consensus can be achieved between opposing factions after a subject has been debated at length. Views soften, an occasional jest by someone round the table smooths the way, dogma is exposed for what it is worth, tempers cool and the contending parties realise that they will not get all they want. A formula is eventually found which satisfies everybody, but it is hard work and I was exhausted after many of the meetings of the Commission. During the three years of the Commission's life, I suffered from minor patches of ill-health and I am sure they were due to worry about some of the divergent attitudes of my fellow Commissioners, and how we were ever going to get a consensus on any topic.

I think one of the things which helped us to reach agreement on most issues was that the Commission adopted as a principle that it would not recommend change for change's sake. Any idiot can propose changes; it costs him nothing and carries no responsibility. The strength of any report lies in the courage to resist the strident clamour of pressure groups and the media, and to propose changes only when they are justified as a result of a careful examination of the relevant facts.

Despite the difficulties I have described, we completed the task in just over three years and reached a surprising measure of unanimity. My friends in the law claim that they have since discovered how this degree of agreement was achieved. A former partner of mine, Brian Jenkins, was addressing a massive gathering of City dignitaries on his election as Sheriff and he told them that he learned from me, early in his career, the secret of success in professional life. He claims that as a young chartered accountant he came to discuss a difficult problem with me and that after a few minutes I said, 'Jenkins, unless you agree with me we shan't make any progress.' I do not remember the incident but it sounds probable. The Commission's work was in fact conducted, for the most part, on more traditional lines.

We held seventy-four meetings which usually lasted a day, and numerous meetings of committees. We received over 3,000 submissions of written evidence. One hundred and fifty-five people gave oral evidence including, on one day, the Chief Justices of America, Australia (Sir Garfield Barwick, mentioned earlier on page 131) and New Zealand. Altogether we made 369 recommendations. Two of the written submissions left a lasting impression on me but for different reasons. The first was commendably short and a pleasure to read for that reason. It said: 'Abolish all lawyers.' The writer did not give his name but gave a number and his address which was Borstal. The other submission said: 'Adopt Magna Carta.' This did not seem any more sensible than the first, but never having read the document I thought it might be interesting to do so and eventually a translation from the Latin was found. The importance of the submission became apparent at chapter 40, which is surely one of the greatest sentences ever written: 'To no one will we sell, to no one will we deny or delay right or justice.' The Commission's work endorsed that profound principle which was laid down nearly eight hundred years ago. Unhappily we found as our work progressed, that it is not observed in the United Kingdom. There were sometimes shocking delays in bringing cases to trial and people were denied rights or justice in some instances because they did not have the means to obtain the advice of lawyers or to pursue their rights in court or in tribunals.

The terms of reference divided our work into two broad categories. The first was legal aid and legal services for the public at large. The second was the affairs of the profession of lawyers. Our researches showed that well-to-do people, and those engaged in commerce and industry and in central and local government, who needed legal services, knew how to set about obtaining them and felt that they received good value for money. In the City of London the quality of legal services plays a part in maintaining this country as in international centre of commerce and finance and contributes to our invisible earnings. The deficiency lies in the considerable number of the population who are less well-to-do and who are not sophisticated in legal matters because they do not often require the services of lawyers. They do not know how to set about finding a lawyer; they show some anxiety in seeking a lawyer's advice, partly because of the unknown and partly because of the fear of cost and an uncertain knowledge of the extent to which they can be helped by legal aid. Our reaction to this was to see how best we could ensure that the less well-to-do could be put in touch with lawyers and get the full benefit of the services they provide.

At the beginning of the report we therefore laid down the principles which we thought should be observed on the subject of the provision of legal services for the public. We said that 'financial assistance out of public funds should be available for every individual who, without it, would suffer an undue financial burden in properly pursuing or defending his legal rights'. In effect, we endorsed chapter 40 of Magna Carta. We believed that the opportunity of the citizen to establish his rights under the law was a basic principle of a free society and without it democracy itself was at risk. That was the theme throughout our report in dealing with the provision of legal services for the public. I doubt whether this was ever appreciated by those members of the public who studied the report. I expected it to be highlighted in the press and quoted as a basic principle on which legal aid should be based but to the best of my recollection it was seldom, if ever, mentioned. I was glad to see, however, that in 1988 the committee under the chairmanship of Lady Marre, which was appointed to consider a number of outstanding problems affecting the legal profession, quoted the above definition with approval.

The second major category which we had to enquire into was the affairs of the legal profession itself. From my point of view this was not difficult. The problems of one profession are very like another. I had spent my life in the accountancy profession so, on a great many topics, I was on familiar ground.

The general public had a particular interest in three

matters. The first was whether the two branches of the legal profession, barristers and solicitors, should be fused into one. On this subject the Commission was unanimous – that the balance of advantages was against fusion. The division between the two branches had evolved over the years and had proved itself in practice; we thought it was likely to continue to be more efficient than a fused profession.

The subject was closely argued in the report. We noticed that responsible witnesses from overseas with practical experience of both systems favoured a two-branch profession. Warren Burger, the Chief Justice of America, was emphatic on this point and, in the course of his oral evidence to the Commission said this:

> My observation from sitting in trial of cases in the *nisi prius* court (Court of First Instance) was that something less than half the lawyers who appeared there were minimally qualified to perform their function . . . Over a long period of time I undertook to take soundings in state courts and in federal courts throughout the country, and the most pessimistic view was that only 25 per cent of the lawyers appearing in our courts were really qualified to represent their clients properly, and to move the case along adequately. Some judges placed it as high as 75 per cent. Somewhere near the midway mark is probably correct and it will vary to some extent from place to place.

The Chief Justice told us that cases were dealt with in British courts more quickly than in America and went on:

> From time to time I have been asked how I account for this. It is not easy to account for it, but an over-simplification perhaps is that in your courts generally you have three experts, who have all been trained in the same tradition and in the same pattern. The judge, almost by definition, has been one of the leading members of the Bar, and the two advocates appearing before him are

trained in the same way the judge was trained. This is not so on our side . . . The trial of the case resembles in a way a three-legged stool. If any of the legs is very much shorter than the others you have not got a very good stool . . . In our system, unfortunately, too often all three of the legs of the stool are not as competent as they should be . . . Even if you have a very experienced judge and he has two mediocre, badly trained or untrained advocates before him, he has difficulty.

The Chief Justice of Australia, Sir Garfield Barwick, confirmed this view and, in the light of his experience of what had occurred in the different states in Australia, said this:

Q Chief Justice, you said that some of the states which were originally fused had become divided and that you had seen this happen. As a consequence of the division, do you think that the quality of the advocacy has improved.

A Yes, it has. That I can say. I have watched these Bars grow in my time as a practising man but even more so since I have been in this office which I have now held for 13 years.

Sir Robin Cook, who was then a judge of the New Zealand court of appeal, gave the following evidence on this point:

I am one of those who does subscribe to this concept of a separate Bar and I make no secret of the fact that I think it is one of the great British achievements to have evolved such a system or institution. One would be somewhat dismayed to find that in the country of its birth it was either abolished or radically altered. I think that the idea of an independent body of men and women, specialists and skilled in their type of legal services, and not mere paid agents for the clients but recognising that they owe some responsibility to the courts, and the standard of ethics and professional skill that tends to go with that, is an extremely valuable concept, and long may that continue.

Another factor which affected the Commission's views on fusion was the point which was stressed throughout the report – there is an increasing need for specialisation in all professions in order to give the best service to the public. In that respect we felt fusion would be a retrograde step. Our endorsement of the two-branch profession did not mean that we thought improvements in the structure and organisation of both branches was unnecessary. We made many proposals which we believed would improve efficiency and reduce costs of operation, some of which have since been adopted.

The second subject which was of special public interest was conveyancing. The solicitor's participation in the process was thoroughly and objectively examined by the Commission and the majority of us considered that conveyancing should remain the responsibility of trained and responsible lawyers. The reason was that it was in the public interest that those who wanted conveyancing and its related work done should employ people who were trained in those subjects and could give the necessary service; who could provide the necessary assurances of integrity; and who could exercise proper care of other people's money. We did not accept the doctrine that anyone could do the job. There is also a fundamental point of principle involved. The whole object of a profession is to ensure that people with the appropriate skills are available to serve the public. This involves a long training and continuing constraints. It serves no purpose to maintain these arduous disciplines, and professional people cannot be expected to undergo them, if at the same time the door is opened and unskilled persons are allowed to do the same work.

Most of the witnesses who advocated opening conveyancing to a free for all destroyed their own arguments by proposing that the laymen who were to be allowed to undertake conveyancing in the future should be trained and put under constraints similar to those which applied to solicitors. This would merely create a quasi-lawyer of second-rate quality who had a limited and insufficient knowledge and the ability to meet only one of the many needs of potential clients. The majority of the Commission felt that this would debase rather than raise standards and this could not be in the public interest. At the time of our report there were between 6,000 and 7,000 firms of solicitors in practice and partners in most of them were capable of undertaking conveyancing, so it was misleading to speak of a monopoly, particularly if, as we proposed, there was greater freedom of advertising and the public were able to shop around.

A minority on the Commission took a different view. They felt that it was wrong for the legal profession to have what they regarded as a monopoly. They felt that if the doors were opened to competition it would lead to a streamlining of procedures and the cost of the conveyancing process would be reduced materially.

The controversy continued long after the report was published and, if the solicitors' branch of the profession had been vigorous in increasing efficiency and in streamlining administration and procedures, I think the majority view of the Commission would have continued to prevail. But solicitors unwisely did not take the action which was urged on them quickly enough. A few years later the government bowed to public opinion and legislation was passed bringing the profession of conveyancers into being. The number of people who are qualified to act in this capacity is, so far, small.

The third subject which was of interest to the public was the desirability of extending the solicitor's right of audience. The Commission laid down as a principle that, in any profession, a restrictive practice must be shown to be in the public interest. The main issue was a proposal that solicitors should have a right of audience in all cases listed for trial by a circuit judge, deputy court judge or recorder. It was not claimed that solicitors should have a right of audience in civil cases before a High Court judge in open Court nor before a High Court judge in the Crown Court.

Here again the pros and cons were closely argued in the Commissioners' report and, subject to varying notes of dissent by some Commissioners, we reached the conclusion by a majority that it would not be in the public interest to extend the solicitor's right of audience in the Crown Court. This view has so far prevailed but it is under constant attack by some members of the solicitors' branch of the profession. The controversy has been stimulated on the grounds that solicitors will lose work as a result of the new profession of conveyancers and that one means of replacing it is to extend the solicitor's right of audience. This does not seem to be a valid argument. The test is not what will be to the advantage of solicitors but what will be of advantage to the public at large, particularly accused persons who are at risk of conviction by a jury and of custodial sentences.

This controversy is unfortunate. It does little for the public image if there is bickering and dissent within a profession and it creates tensions which do nothing but harm.

Another matter which we felt important to spell out in our report was that any profession, to justify its privilege of serving the public in a particular sphere, should ensure as far as possible that the quality of its members' work was satisfactory. This duty lay not only on individual practitioners, but on the governing body or bodies of the profession. We made many proposals which we thought would be helpful, including the introduction of written professional standards (like those used in my profession), post-qualification education and a tightening of the disciplinary procedures. For this, and other reasons, we were unanimously opposed to partnerships by lawyers with members of other professions, such as accountants and estate agents. I notice that this subject has again become a matter of controversy in the solicitors' branch of the profession and it is, I believe, an example of dogma taking precedence over common sense. If it is introduced in due course it will, I am sure, reduce the quality and independence of the legal profession's services to the public.

The last recommendation which was made in the report was probably the most important of all. Much of the evidence we received related to the substance and procedures of the law and the administration of justice, rather than the provision of legal services; all that material fell outside our terms of reference. We concluded that if any real progress was to be made in developing a legal system which was less expensive and time-consuming, those matters should receive attention. We believed that the time had come for a full appraisal of procedures and of the operation in practice of our system of justice in civil and criminal courts. We therefore listed all the matters which had been brought to our attention in a separate appendix and urged that a programme should be drawn up for the purpose of examining in depth each of the proposals and for giving effect to those which would bring about an improvement. I need hardly say that the recommendation was ignored and I have views to express on this subject at the end of this chapter. At the present time, which is nearly ten years later, it has become evident to a growing number of influential people, in and outside the legal profession and the practice of the law, that our legal system, both civil and criminal, needs overhaul. It is ponderous, slow and costly. Steps are now being taken to bring about changes which will doubtless bring improvements in train, such as the Criminal Justice Acts of 1987 and 1988 and the Civil Justice Review. But I am sure a great many years will pass before all the points included in the appendix are properly examined if, indeed, they are examined at all.

Before the Commission completed its work there were indications that efforts would be made to denigrate the report when it was published by claiming that insufficient research had been undertaken. One reason for this was that the Commission was known not to have been impressed by some of the assertions and immature proposals for change, disguised as evidence, which were submitted to us. The complaint of a lack of research has no foundation as anyone will discover who cares to read the 1,600 pages contained in the four volumes of the report; to examine the 101 tables of statistics; and to absorb the 23 separate studies which we instituted. Another reason for this attitude of criticism is that lawyers are not popular by reason of the nature of their calling and some sections of the public were hoping that radical and far-reaching recommendations would be made which would destroy or change the structure of the legal profession. As we expected, the report got a bad press and there was an orchestrated movement by some factions to ensure that this should be so. I held a press conference at which an aggressive reporter said, 'Why did you not make some of the radical recommendations which are necessary?' I said, 'What radical recommendations have you in mind?' He remained silent, and to the embarrassment of some of his colleagues, and the pleasure of others, could not remember any of them.

On the day of publication the BBC asked for a television recording for the 9 o'clock news that night which I was glad to provide. The producer came to lunch beforehand at the offices of the Commission and said that he would not indicate the questions he was going to ask as he preferred spontaneous answers. As soon as the cameras began to whirr it became obvious that the producer had not read the report or, indeed, the summary of recommendations which were included at the end for easy reading; his questions were, I thought, loaded if not biased and he was obviously out of his depth. My answers became increasingly acerbic and finally I said that if he really wanted to know what the report was about I would tell him the questions to ask and then I would give the replies. The camera crew did not conceal their enjoyment at this exchange of pleasantries. The cameras stopped and the producer, with an ill grace, took down in manuscript a number of questions which I dictated to him, the answers to which would have indicated the main theme of the report and its general objectives. The cameras began to whirr afresh and, on the new basis, we got along fairly well. When the programme appeared that night virtually all this material had been cut out and the recording put before the public bore no resemblance to what had taken place during the afternoon.

Various studies of the effects of Royal Commission reports have been made and one of them came to the conclusion that it often took about fifty years before the major recommendations were put in train. This is not as surprising as it sounds. One effect of a Royal Commission report, if not one of its purposes, is to make people think – not only the people who read the final report but the large number of people who have to prepare written and oral evidence for it. As a result of this process it is often realised that present procedures or policies need overhaul. There is, however, a natural inertia and a resistance to make changes, even changes for the better and the period which elapses before anything emerges often covers years. One example is given earlier in this chapter where I pointed out that our civil and criminal procedures needed overhaul. Now, some ten years later, something (but probably not enough) is being done about it. But it will be years before they are finally adopted and put into force.

The legal profession, and those engaged in the practice of the law, gave the report a good reception. Although they were content with the main recommendations there was no great enthusiasm to put any of them into force, though some of them have been adopted. The report is now often quoted as a reliable authority for the way ahead.

I feel some resentment at the attitude of successive governments to the reports made by Royal Commissions and other similar committees which they, or their predecessors, appoint. Such bodies involve a great deal of time, effort and money on the part of a large number of people, but on publication nothing emerges from the government of the day saying what their intentions are. The cost of our Royal Commission was just under £1¼ million, but this represents only a very small part of the total cost. There is the time expended by literally hundreds of persons who, without remuneration, are involved in producing evidence or otherwise taking part in the Commissions' work in one form or another. I feel that, out of courtesy alone, the government of the day should, within a year of publication, issue a statement with reasons, of the recommendations it accepts, those it rejects and those which are deferred.

This subject became a matter of public interest in 1981 and correspondence took place in *The Times*. I contributed to this correspondence, in the course of which I made the following comments:

The two branches of the legal profession have been active in following up the recommendations (i.e. of the Royal Commission on Legal Services) but the government's attitude has been noticeably supine. The legal profession is being impeded by the lack of action by government and, without some thrust from that source, much harm will be done. The whole purpose of the Royal Commission's work was to bring about improvements – some of them long overdue – in the provision of legal services for the public and in simplifying cumbersome legal procedures; this purpose is in danger of being frustrated.

The complaints now raised in your correspondence columns are of very long standing. The last authoritative report on Royal Commissions was completed in 1910 and was addressed to the then Home Secretary, Mr Winston Churchill MP. Most of its recommendations (which even today are wholly in point) are still ignored both in the method of appointment and the follow-up procedure. It makes the following specific comment, among many others which repay study.

'We are unanimous in believing that the appointment of Royal Commissions is useful for the elucidation of difficult subjects which are attracting public attention but in regard to which the information is not sufficiently accurate to form a preliminary to legislation. That this view is generally held is obvious from the fact that the number of Royal Commissions has been greatly increased in recent years but we have some doubts whether in all cases the practical results achieved have been commensurate with the time, labour and expense involved and we are disposed to deprecate the appointment of Royal Commissions on subjects as to which there is no reasonable prospect of early legislation.'

Belatedly in 1983, four years after it was published, the government issued a White Paper on the Royal Commission's report which expressed reservations on some points but gave general approval to all the principal recommendations. In 1987 a new Lord Chancellor was appointed in the person of Lord Mackay of Clashfern. In January 1989 three Green Papers were issued as discussion documents under his authority, proposing that all the main recommendations in the Royal Commission's report, which had been approved by the government in the 1983 White Paper, should be overturned. This astonishing *volte-face* raised much controversy. The Green Papers were crudely prepared and presented, without adequate consultation with interested parties, without proper research, and without the benefit of practical experience. They set aside a period of three months only for submissions and comment, and this short time limit was also the subject of strong criticism.

Lawyers do not belong to a popular profession, and some of the less well-informed media welcomed the Green Papers as a great breakthrough; they regarded them as a welcome reform of a profession which they claimed was out of date and surrounded by unnecessary restrictions and privileges. Different views were expressed by people and organisations who were familiar with the legal process and had occasion to use legal services in the normal course of their work; by the judiciary; and by a large number of lawyers of integrity, who had spent virtually the whole of their professional lives in the administration of justice. All condemned the Green

Papers with varying degrees of emphasis. On 7 April 1989 an historic debate took place in the House of Lords, which began at 9.30 in the morning and ended at 10.30 that evening. Over fifty peers, including myself, spoke in the debate, and the overwhelming burden of their speeches was to condemn the proposals.

The main points of controversy in this debate centred round the following issues:

- The effect of the Green Papers was to destroy the independence or the legal profession and place it under the dominance of the government.
- A large number of paralegal organisations would be brought within the same net and placed under the dominance of the government. (The paralegals are persons who give some legal advice for reward as part of their ordinary business or who engage in advocacy. For example, accountants give some legal advice on taxation matters, and the trade unions represent their members in industrial tribunals.)
- Partnerships between barristers and solicitors would be permitted, which would, in the course of time, result in fusion of the two branches of solicitors and barristers respectively.
- The effect of fusion would be to damage, if not destroy, the existence of a strong and independent bar.
- Fusion, coupled with freedom for banks and building societies to undertake conveyancing business, would sound the death knell of a large number of small solicitors in all parts of the country.
- Multidisciplinary partnerships would be permitted which would allow solicitors to practise in partnership with other professions, such as estate agents and accountants.
- The quality of the judiciary would be debased and its independence impaired.
- Contingency fees, which are regarded by many responsible lawyers as a nursery for corruption, would be

permitted under certain conditions.

- The real need is not to tamper with the structure of the legal profession, but to review the whole process of the law, which is slow, costly and, in many respects, not up to date.

By seeking to impose the political dogma of 'competition' on the legal profession, the government has upset some of the basic principles on which justice in this country has hitherto been based. In Chapter 5 I indicated the nine characteristics of a profession. If the proposals in the Green Papers are put into effect they will destroy, as regards the legal profession, most of those nine characteristics.

At the time of writing it is not clear what the outcome will be. The government has a large majority in the House of Commons and, by the exercise of a three-line whip, can secure a majority in the Lords. The Prime Minister and her Lord Chancellor may be determined to use these powers to force the proposals through both Houses. I hope it will not be so, because I believe, with unshakeable conviction, that it will damage irreparably the cause of justice in this country.

Some years ago at a meeting with the head of the Treasury, Sir William Armstrong (later Lord Armstrong of Sanderstead) told me that he had watched many governments come and go in the course of his lifetime, and had learned that they were ultimately defeated by their friends and not by the opposition. The infighting and backbiting which always goes on in politics, and the formulation of inconsistent and ill-considered measures based on political dogma as opposed to common sense, were the invariable causes of their downfall. I have a profound admiration for the record of the Conservative government in the past ten years, which has raised the country out of the morass in which it was wallowing, but imprudent proposals such as those proposed in the Green Papers are a typical example of measures which antagonise some of the government's best friends.

While the controversy was raging, I was asked by the

Oxford Union Society and the Union Society at Cambridge whether I would lead debates in both places opposing the adoption of the Green Papers. I did so, and attended at Oxford and Cambridge within a few days of each other. It was a new experience, which I enjoyed. I did not have a great deal of preparation to undertake because I was able to draw on the issues which had been exposed in the debate in the House of Lords. At Oxford the House rejected the papers as being a 'threat to justice'. At Cambridge the House rejected them outright.

Lord Rothschild was the chairman of the Royal Commission on Gambling 1976-78. We met from time to time in the City and found that we had common views on the way in which Royal Commissions should be appointed and how they should be organised and operated. We therefore jointly published in 1980 a 'Memorial' on the subject. It was a useful adjunct to the report made by Mr Churchill in 1910 and supported many of the views expressed in it. I do not suppose that anybody has since paid any attention to the Memorial, which is disappointing, because it provides some useful guidance born of hard practical experience.

On completion of their reports, the chairmen of Royal Commissions are sometimes made life peers. I was so appointed in the Honours List of 1 January 1981.

11.

The House of Lords 1981 to Date

I do not know how other new peers react when they move to the House of Lords, but I experienced many different emotions: pride at being able to take part in Parliament; excitement at the prospect of a new activity; anxiety as to what sort of figure I would cut in debate; pleasure in joining what is a comfortable and sociable club; overall, a feeling of satisfaction at the end of many years of hard work. When I was at a nursery school in Johannesburg at the age of about 5, I remember being taunted by my school-fellows on some trivial subject. I shouted, 'When I grow up I am going to be King.' Enraged by further ridicule, and in an effort to keep my end up, I shouted, 'Well then, I shall be a Lord.' It has taken about eighty years to realise what that involves.

The occasion seemed to call for some celebration and we had a family dinner party to which one or two special friends were invited. At the end of it my elder son, Peter, who has a skill with words, recited the following ditty. The gentle irony, which poked fun at so many aspects of the City which I had watched all my life, gave me pleasure.

City Ditty

Now this tells the tale of the City
  As old and as true as the sky
And the clerk that shall heed it shall prosper
  But the clerk that ignores it shall cry.

At the top of the heap sit the bankers
  To every large deal they're alive
You may purchase advice in their boardrooms
  Provided you leave them by five

And then we must turn to the lawyers
    So secure in their Courts and their Inns
Pay to consult them the first time
    Or they'll charge ten times more for your sins.

And of course there are always the brokers
    Who'll peddle you stock at a word
And seduce you with over large lunches
    Which conceal that the price is absurd.

Outside on the fringes are lurking
    Oh beware of the Revenue men
With statutes, back tax and assessments
    Which they serve with an unctuous grin.

Just beyond the Square Mile lies Whitehall
    With index linked pensions for all
And endless politeness in dealings
    Although every decision they'll stall.

And brooding as always above it
    The Old Lady with basilisk stare
They refer to the Street as Threadneedle
    But perhaps they should call it Threadbare.

In this jungle of sharks and of con men
    Our clerk may give way to despair
Should he ever forget for a moment
    That the chartered accountant is there.

In the legends they tell in the City
    Such men have no heart and fish eyes
All life is a balanced trial balance
    And figures alone tell no lies.

But the clerk who has eyes for to see with
    Will discern that the truth is not so
For the chartered accountant will serve you
    To whatever the lengths he must go.

Now virtue is seldom rewarded
  But tonight there is virtue to cheer
For by leave of Her Majesty's Government
  We can still make a CA a peer.

I was introduced in the Lords on 11 February 1981 and took my seat on the Cross Benches. I have never been strongly politically orientated though my natural leanings veer to the Right rather than the Left. I prefer to remain unfettered so that I can express my opinions in the House unaffected by any political affiliations. One of the characteristics of an auditor is that he should at all times be independent and free to express his opinion without fear or favour. This is a precious privilege and I think has been ingrained in me for so long that I would be reluctant to take the whip for any political party.

As mentioned later, the total membership of the House of Lords is about 1,200 and of these some 350 are life peers. There can be no possible justification for manning the upper chamber of Parliament by hereditary peers and, if we had to start again, it is inconceivable that such a system would ever be thought of. There is an argument in logic for manning the upper Chamber with life peers because many of them have achieved distinction and experience as a condition of their appointment to the peerage. Nevertheless, the system works surprisingly well. The relatively small number of hereditary peers who take an active part in the Lords are often in the younger age groups and they do so for the best reason in the world – that it interests them and they have a wish to discharge their responsibilities. Life peers are in an older bracket so that there is a good balance of ages. On any subject which is brought forward for debate there is usually at least one hereditary or life peer, and often many, who can speak with real authority and experience. This is invaluable in arriving at balanced conclusions. There is another reason why the system works. There are occasional exceptions but on the whole everyone in the Lords is polite. Politeness reigns inside and outside the Chamber and in the committees and subcommittees which are appointed to consider various topics and to make reports. It astonished me after my experience on the Royal Commission on Legal Services to sit on committees in the Lords without being able to detect, from the way they spoke, what the political affiliations of the members happened to be. With few exceptions, members seek to be objective and to express their views with moderation. I think that this atmosphere in the House is one of the things that has given me the greatest pleasure since I was given the privilege of taking part in its affairs. The behaviour in the Commons on some occasions and, particularly at question time, is shaming and a shocking example to the public at large; it is in complete contrast to that prevailing in the Lords.

Another advantage is that their lordships have more time than members of the House of Commons and they are able to sift Bills in detail. Their work in committee, which comprises the whole House, is careful and painstaking and often more thorough than in the lower Chamber. This is particularly important at the present time, because in recent years a number of important Bills have been presented to Parliament in a crude and unfinished state with the result that a large number of amendments have to be made by the government in the committee stage. The responsibility for this indifferent administration rests firmly on the Minister who sponsors the Bill when it is first introduced and the staff in his department. Excuses are sometimes made that the defects are due to a shortage of time but the consequential effect is that the time of a large number of people and much expense are wasted in correcting the defects which would not be necessary if the job had been done properly in the first place.

Those are some of the reasons why the procedures in the Lords are important. Some debates are, of course, boring but usually they are conducted with good humour and without rudeness. They tend to express balanced and sensible views which is the ideal approach for an upper Chamber. Everyone knows that the power and policy rests with the

Commons who have the final say, but when the Lords takes a strong view on an important subject, the government of the day takes notice and is usually reluctant to overturn it. I have no doubt that efforts will continue to change the constitution of the upper Chamber or to abolish it. So long as both Houses continue to conduct their business in the present fashion there appears to be merit in leaving things as they are.

The everyday administration within the House of Lords is efficient. Hansard, which records the day's proceedings and the answers to written questions, is printed during the night and is distributed by special delivery, to reach the addresses of peers in London by 8 am the following day. If the proceedings go on late into the night, anything which takes place after about 9 pm is incorporated at the beginning of the following day's Hansard. When Hansard is delivered it is accompanied by a separate detailed agenda for the proceedings which will take place on that day. This paper also gives a forecast agenda for several succeeding days. By this means, peers can adjust their diaries to fit in their other activities.

The total membership of the Lords is about twelve hundred, but not more than three hundred can be regarded as being regular in their attendance and in voting in the divisions. This compares with the membership in the Commons of six hundred and fifty. Between twenty and thirty bishops are members of the House ex officio, and one of them takes prayers each day. Their membership ceases when they retire from office. There are also normally twelve Lords of Appeal in Ordinary who represent the highest judicial tribunal in the United Kingdom. They sit on the Cross Benches, in order to maintain their independence and freedom from political pressure. They continue as members of the House after they have retired from office. The bishops and Law Lords are included in the figure of twelve hundred.

Each day's proceedings begin with question time, and these sessions are always well attended because the questions open up discussion on a wide variety of current topics and also give indications of government policy. In the normal way only four questions are put each day which take up about half and hour. If any one question begins to take up an excessive amount of time the Leader of the House steps in and suggests that we should move on to the next topic. Question time is followed by second readings or other debates or by the committee stage of a Bill. There is a considerable exodus of peers after question time and unless the subject under debate is of special interest, the number of peers who sit in the Chamber at any one time is seldom more than one hundred and often a good deal less.

Until I joined the House I had not realised how quickly the proceedings can expose the qualities and personalities of individuals. The heavyweights stand out clearly and the House fills when they are speaking. Peers of lighter metal, and the recognised bores, empty the Chamber quickly. Those who leave the Chamber attend to their own affairs in their own rooms (if they hold office) or in the library, and only emerge when a division is called. Ministers in office who, in question time and in debate, deal with the matters under discussion clearly and succinctly, and with good humour, establish themselves as candidates for higher office. Those who fail are dropped in the next government reshuffle. It is a hard school, but a good one.

The influence wielded by the Cross Benchers is not unimportant and the government is sensitive to their attitude. They number about two hundred and fifty out of the total of twelve hundred, but only fifty can be regarded as regular in their attendance. Some of them lean to the Right and others to the Left but they are all independent in outlook. Although the Conservative peers are in the majority in the upper Chamber, it is surprising how often the government is defeated by the combined strength of the Labour and Liberal peers, with the support of some of the Cross Benchers.

The Select Committee of the House of Lords appoints subcommittees to examine particular topics. The subcommittees, usually about fifteen in number, are drawn from all shades of opinion, and peers are normally chosen because their past record is likely to enable them to make a positive contribution to the matter in hand. I have sat for some years on a subcommittee which, as a routine, examines finance, economics and regional policy in the European Community, but I have also sat from time to time on others.

The secretarial services for the subcommittees are provided by permanent staff and there is also as a rule a 'special adviser', who has detailed knowledge of the matter under discussion and is able to assist the secretariat in drafting the reports. The witnesses who are invited to give evidence comprise government ministers, members of the European Parliament, industrialists, bankers, academics and others, all of whom are specialists in their own fields. The reports are of high quality and, as each report is completed, it is made available to the public and usually time is set aside for a debate upon it in the House. The reports relating to the European Community do not attract much attention from the public in the United Kingdom but they are widely read abroad, partly because we are the only member State which provides a regular service of this kind.

Subcommittees, usually comprising five peers drawn from different parts of the House, are also appointed to scrutinise and formulate amendments to private Bills before they come before the House. This is a time-consuming task, but it is a valuable service which in the long term saves a great deal of parliamentary time.

Unlike the Commons, no remuneration is paid to peers either for attendance in the House or for work on Select Committees; they are, however, reimbursed for travelling and subsistence expenditure.

Any peer who wished to devote his whole life to the House of Lords would have no difficulty in doing so. The volume of paperwork which goes through every day is enormous and one could spend all the working hours keeping abreast of it and taking part in debates when a Bill is in committee. I try to keep my speeches short but, as everyone knows, the shorter the speech the more time it takes in preparation. I speak only on matter of which I have specialised knowledge or a particular interest, such as Legal Aid, the Criminal Justice Bill, the Insolvency Bill, Company Law, the appointment of non-executive directors to the boards of companies, matters affecting the legal profession, Sunday sports and debates on reports by Select Committees of which I have been a member.

Except during the War, I have never in my life been up all night, but on one occasion in 1988 I sat through a debate on the Education Reform Bill on which a division took place the following morning. The amendment was designed to provide financial assistance for English schools in the European Community which have been long established and are well respected. Many United Kingdom citizens from all walks of life are now required to work in the Community in connection with our increasing industrial and commercial interests there. It is sometimes difficult to persuade them to leave the United Kingdom and one of their main anxieties is that their children will be able to receive an education when abroad which will enable them without difficulty to enter schools, universities and polytechnics when they return to this country. Some of the other member states are already far-sighted enough to provide assistance of this sort for their citizens who work outside their own country. The necessary amendment to the Bill was duly passed by twenty-four votes to twenty-one at the unseemly hours of 8.12 am, but unhappily the government took care to have the amendment reversed in the Commons.

Early in 1988 a subcommittee, of which I became a member, was set up to consider the question of fraud and irregularity (referred to for short as fraud) in the European Community, and its report made startling disclosures. The annual income and the expenditure of the Community is about £25 billion, and these are not large sums compared with the annual turnover of some of our great international industrial corporations. Most of the revenue and the expenditure take place in the twelve member states and that is where the bulk of the fraud arises.

These are a summary of the Select Committee's findings:

- Fraud in all the member states is known to be rife and this has gone on, unchecked, for many years.
- No Community institution has ever attempted to quantify the amount of fraud. Various estimates suggest a figure of plus or minus 10 per cent of the budget. Figures of £2-6 billion each year have been quoted in the media.
- The causes of fraud in the Community were analysed and it emerged that virtually all the long-established rules for good financial administration were applied either loosely or not at all. The Committee found over-complicated regulations, excessive proliferation of product classifications, an absence of lucid instructions at the operating levels, inadequate internal controls and internal audit, failure to report fraud, failure to follow up fraud by criminal action or civil claims, inadequate publicity when fraud was established, an absence of trained staff, and inadequate cooperation between officials throughout the Community.
- The obligations imposed on the Court of Auditors by the Treaty of Rome were not being observed, because the Court had neither the resources nor an accepted authority to do so. There was virtually no audit coverage in the member states. Criticisms by the Court in its reports are not followed up adequately or at all.
- Above all, there was an absence of political will in the Community institutions, and in the member states, to check corrupt practices and to prevent a huge waste of public funds.
- The only hope of correcting the situation was to prepare a coordinated programme which would eliminate each of the causes one by one. The Committee estimated that this would take three to five years to implement and that it would require sustained leadership of high quality.

There can seldom have been a more scathing commentary on the administration of any governmental organisation.

There are signs that the Community are at last beginning to take the subject of fraud seriously, and the Select Committee's report has contributed to this awakening. There has been much talk and protestations of good intentions but, in my opinion, it will be years before fraud and irregularity are brought down to an acceptable level.

The numerous studies which have been made in recent years by subcommittees of the Select Committee of the House of Lords, and particularly the enquiry into fraud, have made me increasingly uneasy about the administration of the European Community. Since it first began on 9 May 1950, great strides have been made and much has been achieved. I do not doubt that it was right for the UK to join in 1973 and it is a pity that it did not do so earlier. One half of the total exports of the United Kingdom are now made to the Common Market. The studies show, however, that the administration is often inefficient. One does not have to look far for reasons.

The task of setting up a very large administrative and legislative organisation inevitably takes a long time and, to that extent, the Community is still in its infancy. There are other causes. The basic structure is, in my view, ponderous and transparently inefficient for the job. There are six separate layers and there is also an absence of what Mrs Thatcher describes as 'democratic accountability' which will become of increasing importance if, and when, Stages 2 and 3 of the Delors Plan are put into operation.

1. At the top, there is the European Council, comprising the heads of state and foreign ministers, which meets two or three times a year for the purpose of considering wide policy issues. It does not determine Community legislation.

2. The second layer is the Council of Ministers, which is in effect the main decision-maker for all major issues. It consists of ministers from member state government, who fight their own corners on behalf of the states to which

they belong. Attendance of ministers on the Council depends on the policy under discussion so that, although there is theoretically only one Council, it meets in practice in different compositions (agriculture, finance, transport etc). Decisions in one area of policy are made in isolation from the others. The Council's meetings are not held in public and its proceedings are secret. Members only account *ex post facto* to their national parliaments. The presidency changes every six months. Unanimity is needed for important decisions.

3. The third layer is the Committee of Permanent Representatives (COREPER) which is composed of ambassadors and representatives of member states. Through its own organisation, COREPER prepares the work for most Council sessions and its representatives have considerable influence on the conduct of Community business.

4. The fourth layer is the European Parliament, which has no legislative powers. It comprises 518 members but only about a hundred actually participate in the work of the Parliament and another two hundred attend meetings. It can and does express opinions but has few powers and a unanimous vote by the Council of Ministers remains the last word. Measures which have the force of law, and in many cases apply directly to Community citizens, are made not by the European Parliament, but by the Council of Ministers (and by the Commission where it has decision-making powers).

5. The fifth layer is the European Commission, which carries out the day-to-day work and has the sole power of initiative. It is also the sole authority (aside from the Court) for the valid interpretation of Treaty provisions. Its work is theoretically subject to the surveillance of the European Parliament alone, but the ultimate power of Parliament to enforce its will upon the Commission is only by the unrealistic and draconian step of enforcing the Commission collectively to resign as a result of a two-thirds majority vote of Parliament.

6. The sixth layer comprises the member states, who are responsible for collecting and spending the bulk of the revenues of the Community. The surveillance which can be exerted over the member states by any of the other five layers is limited and, where possible, difficult to apply.

The affairs of the Community are conducted in nine different languages, which involves a huge task of translation. The consequential expenditure of time and overhead expense is enormous; one quarter of the Commission personnel is employed on linguistic work. The risk of misunderstanding or misinterpretation is always present.

Because there are twelve member states, each feels, as a matter of principle, that it must be represented in every phase of the operations. Political manoeuvring takes place as regards the appointments to the different types of operation. This in turn creates delays and increases time and overhead expense.

As the Fraud Report pointed out, the financial and budgetary administration in the member states (where the bulk of the revenue and expenditure arises) is weak. The Court of Auditors has limited resources and even when it makes clear and adverse reports they are not followed up with the vigour which is necessary, if at all. Its audit coverage in the member states is wholly inadequate although fraud and irregularity are acknowledged to be rife. The great industrial undertakings throughout the world conduct their affairs in thousands of billions of pounds each year. Taken as a whole, their operations are seldom tainted with continuous fraud and irregularity, because they are efficiently managed. This is not the case in the operations of the Community.

The mismanagement of the Common Agricultural Policy (CAP), which has been continuing for years, is another example of bad administration. In 1985, 73 per cent of the total Community budget was spent in support for farm prices, modernisation of agriculture and on fisheries, although only nine out of every hundred workers in the Community are employed in agriculture. The creation of unsaleable stocks of goods and the expenditure of large sums in storage is inexcusable. If private enterprise behaved in a similar way, there would be a clamour to introduce legislation to stop or prevent it: because it is carried out by the Community itself, it continues. The comments on CAP in the 1988 report of the UK National Consumer Council are highly critical.

Above all, there is a lack of political will. This is in part created by the complex organisational structure described above. Again and again, decisions which are administratively necessary are deferred or do not take place because they are politically difficult or because the necessary majority is unobtainable.

Unless there is a radical improvement in the existing administration, I am sceptical of the Single European Act and the possibility, by 1992, of the creation of a Europe without frontiers. There has, at the same time, been talk of a single European currency, but I believe this is also unrealistic until the affairs of the Community are controlled by some form of federal government which can manage the economy upon which a single currency necessarily depends. The countries outside the Community are unlikely to have confidence in a currency which can be eroded by the uncoordinated actions of individual members states.

I think that we are attempting to move too quickly and that by doing so we shall defeat our own ends. The danger is that we shall create a ragged and inefficient organisation, which will have gaping holes and wide inconsistencies, and fraud will be worse than it is at present; the public and other nations may then begin to lose confidence in the European Community. In an earlier chapter I said that the misinformed public expects South Africa to achieve in years what can, in practice, only be achieved in centuries, and much the same atmosphere seems to me to prevail about the future of the Community.

I believe that the first task is to correct the existing

deficiencies and I doubt whether this can be fully attained until the basic structure described earlier is put on to a streamlined and more workmanlike basis. It will require a tremendous effort of sustained leadership of high quality – a commodity which is in short supply. At the same time it would be sensible to decide that in a selected year in the future (say, ten or twenty years ahead) the Community operations in Brussels, Luxembourg and Strasbourg will be conducted in not more than two languages (English and French), preferably only in one. Until these steps have been taken, I question whether the present objectives for 1992 can be attained as quickly as has been generally proclaimed. I think it will be deep into the twenty-first century before there is in fact a single European market, involving the removal of cross-border barriers; the harmonisation of legislation and of taxation; the free movement of capital, goods, people and services; the adoption of a single currency and a European bank which exercises the traditional role of a central bank.

The remit given to another subcommittee of which I was a member was 'Relations between the Community and Japan' and its findings exposed some of the reasons why Britain's economic performance since the end of the Second World War has been disappointing.

At the end of the war Germany and Japan were in a deplorable state due to the ravages and deprivations of war and merciless bombing. With the possible exception of the United States, those two countries now have the strongest economies in the world. The quality and extent of their industrial output is remarkable; their currencies are firm and, politically and economically, they are both dominant in world affairs.

Britain suffered greatly during the war, but she was not in anything like the same poor shape as her defeated rivals. In the ten years since she came into office in 1979, Mrs Thatcher has done a great deal to provide the country with a new sense of purpose, but in the last forty five years Britain has lagged behind and her position and influence are being overshadowed. Our balance of payments is dangerously adverse; the currency is erratic and the country is still plagued with outbreaks of strikes and industrial unrest. In 1988 the Gross Domestic Product (expressed per capita of population in thousands of dollars) was 23.3 in Japan, 19.6 in the United States and 14.1 in Britain. Between 1980 and 1986 Japanese GDP grew by an average of 6.6 per cent a year; this compares with 3.2 per cent for the United States and 2.3 per cent for Britain.

The Office of Fair Trading has recently drawn attention to our industrial position and has pointed out that in several sectors of our manufacturing industry the import penetration from abroad – despite the extra burden of transport and handling – exceeds 50 per cent, and that these imports account altogether for some 17 per cent of Britain's manufacturing production. Equally significant is competition from foreign firms operating in the United Kingdom. These account in total for 20 per cent of British manufacturing output and in some sectors for considerably more. Foreign firms employ new methods and techniques which enable them to compete successfully with home-based industrial output. These percentages may escalate when a single European market comes into being in 1992.

The Select Committee ascribed Japan's astonishing recovery and increasing dominance to the following factors and I suggest, if a similar study was made of the situation in Germany, it would arrive at much the same conclusions.

- The Japanese economic machine is growing ever more powerful and it is sustained by continuity in national policy.
- In industrial output Japan's creed is quality of product, quality of presentation and punctuality of delivery.
- Before undertaking any enterprise or project their research is thorough and of a high order.
- In investment projects Japan is willing and able to take a long-term view. British philosophy requires a much shorter timescale for payoff than is the practice in Japan.

- Japan's annual expenditure on research and development is considerable and relatively much greater than that prevailing in Britain.
- Their personnel management is exceptionally good and they pay special attention to the selection of employees and to their subsequent training. They have an ability to motivate staff and establish good labour relations. For these reasons the operations of the Unions in the form in which they exist in Britain are of little significance. For example, during our visit to the Japanese Nissan car factory in Sunderland we were told that membership of a union is optional and only 18 per cent of the total work force were members.
- The education system in Japan creates production line workers of good quality.
- By reason of the country's economic success, the Japanese banks are immensely wealthy. Japan at present conducts her overseas lending from London, as being a convenient operating centre, but it was made clear to us that, in the course of time, Tokyo expects to overtake London as a world financial centre.

The evidence given to the Select Committee was that what was best in Britain could match anything produced in Japan. This is encouraging because it means that we are capable of achieving equality of output without slavishly copying the Japanese culture and way of life, which in many ways would not be acceptable in Britain. Britain fails because, at all levels below the best, her achievements are noticeably lower than in Japan. I doubt whether the seriousness of the position is known or recognised by the man in the street in Britain and it is not the sort of material which any Government would wish to emphasise; but if we do not take steps to improve our position, Britain will drop further and further behind. It will need exceptional leadership in every walk of life, and at least a generation, to bring about a significant change – by Government, by the parties in Opposition, by management (comprising the humblest charge-hands on the shop floor up through the foremen, the plant and section managers to the boardrooms), by the Unions, by the media, in the schools and indeed in the upbringing of children in the homes.

A separate book would be needed to define all that could and might be done. I believe that one of the reasons for our decline is our political system and the emphasis on the political doctrine of equality rather than quality. Moreover the political parties are so busy opposing each other's policies and reversing their predecessor's decisions when they come into power, that far too little time is spent on formulating a settled and consistent industrial policy which would enable Britain to retain 'Great' in her name and to keep on level terms with her rivals. We can achieve miracles in Britain if we have a common purpose and good leadership. The last time this occurred began on 3 September 1939, but it ended in the autumn of 1945 when the war ended and we reverted to our normal system of political discord and divergent policies.

12.

Special Assignments 1975 to Date

The Carrian Case (Hong Kong)

The Carrian case involved commercial fraud in Hong Kong. My involvement was as an expert witness from the accountancy profession on behalf of the Hong Kong government and, on and off, this occupied three years from May 1984 to May 1987.

The short life of the Carrian complex began in 1979. The audited accounts showed that it flourished up to the end of 1980 and the audited accounts for 1981 showed that it was still flourishing. By that time, however, there were problems. A liquidity shortage was announced by the directors in October 1982 and total collapse ensued not long afterwards. Criminal proceedings took place against two of the directors, Tan and Ho, and against Begg and Lo, a partner and manager respectively of the auditors, Price Waterhouse, one of the eight largest firms of international accountants usually referred to as the 'Big Eight'. At a later stage the two Lam brothers were joined as defendants.

The allegations related to 1981 in connection with a company listed on the Hong Kong Stock Exchange called Carrian Investments Ltd (CIL). Tan, the chairman, owned 55 per cent of the shares of CIL through a private company which he owned called Carrian Holdings Ltd (CHL) and the public, together with Tan and his associates, held the other 45 per cent of the shares. Tan also owned or directed a number of other private companies which were not part of either CIL or CHL.

The charge alleged that all the accused had conspired together, as a result of which the published audited accounts for 1981 were false and misleading. The audit report on the accounts was 'clean' and contained no qualifications.

The details of the charge were simple in character and fell into three categories. At that time the rate of exchange of Hong Kong dollars was approximately ten dollars to the pound sterling.

1. Five transactions were entered into by CIL, giving rise to profits of $312 million, which were included in normal trading profits for 1981. The Crown alleged that these were contrived transactions with related parties at artificial prices, not at arm's length and entered into with CHL or other Tan companies which made corresponding losses. It was alleged that these were not normal profits and should have been disclosed as extraordinary items in CIL's published account for 1981.

2. A number of shares held by CIL in a Hong Kong bank were sold for a profit of $312 million in the last few hours of 31 December 1981 to a company owned and directed by the Lam brothers. A condition of the sale was that the Lam brothers should make a deposit in cash of $144 million and provide a bank guarantee for the remaining instalments of the purchase price, amounting to $337 million. The deposit was never paid and the bank guarantee was never provided; the shares in the Hong Kong bank were never delivered to the Lams and stamp duty was never paid on the sale. The Crown alleged that the sale of the shares was never completed and the profit should not have been included in CIL's profit and loss account for 1981 at all.

3. At 31 December 1981 assets belonging to CIL amounting to $773 million had been removed without authority and pledged to secure liabilities of CHL or some other Tan private companies. The Crown alleged that the accounts of CIL for 1981 should have disclosed that assets of that amount were not in the control and custody of CIL.

Some of the relevant facts and figures are as follows:

- the total number of documents seized by the police at the beginning of the case was estimated to be between one and one and a half million;
- the committal proceedings before a magistrate lasted over six months and the trial in the High Court, which began on 19 February 1986, lasted nineteen months (the defence not being called upon);
- over one hundred witnesses were called by the prosecution; some gave evidence in Chinese;
- the number of exhibits at the trial was over five thousand;
- the transcripts in the trial in the High Court covered over 25,000 pages;
- the Court did not sit after lunch; in practice it was in session for no more than three and a half hours a day, sometimes less;
- there were two expert witnesses on behalf of the Crown; Eoghan McMillan, the senior partner of Arthur Andersen & Co in Hong Kong, and myself. The time which elapsed between the beginning and end of the evidence of some witnesses at the trial was very long. In the case of Eoghan McMillan it was eight weeks and in my own case it was seven weeks;
- in that period of seven weeks, I was in the box for twenty days and answered some six thousand questions. I referred to over four hundred exhibits. Eoghan McMillan answered more questions than I did;
- the total cost of the case from first to last, under all heads of expenditure, has never come to light, but my guess from figures quoted to me from time to time is somewhere between £20 and £30 million.

At times during the trial the health of the judge, Mr Justice Barker, was not good and he appeared to find the trial burdensome. In the latter months he took no notes and he confessed to Counsel that he was behind in his reading of the transcripts; for these reasons it would have been impossible for him to prepare a proper summing up at the end of the trial. The case was conducted more in the nature of a friendly civil arbitration than a criminal trial. The accused, if they wished to attend Court, sat with their defending Counsel, who were in different parts of the Court, some in the back rows, which meant that voices had to be raised so that Counsel and witnesses could hear each other. The accused were excused from attending Court if they did not wish to do so. The Lam brothers, for practical purposes, did not attend throughout the nineteen months of the trial. Tan and Ho were absent for months on end.

The jury were absent from Court for long periods for the reason that lengthy applications or submissions were made to the judge by defence Counsel which the jury were not permitted to hear. Apart from this, even when in Court, the jury were continually sent out for long or short periods while submission of one sort or another were made to the judge. The prolixity of counsel was at times extravagant and cross-examination unduly prolonged.

My job as an expert witness was, of course, not to express any view or opinions as to whether there had been conspiracy between the accused or whether the indictment was correctly drawn. I was asked to explain what the normal functions and procedures of an audit were and whether, in my opinion, the accounts of CIL for 1981, as presented, were true and fair. My evidence was clear that in my opinion they were not, and that the audit report should have been heavily qualified by drawing attention to the transactions which I have described. The evidence I was required to present to the Court gave me no difficulty because I had been engaged on and off on that type of work ever since I was 17 years old. Eoghan McMillan and I prepared our evidence independently of each other, but in substance what we said was identical.

In the course of the trial the judge made a number of rulings affecting the evidence which could be given by Eoghan McMillan and myself. We found that these rulings were difficult to interpret; at times they were contradictory and this added greatly to the work we both had to put into the case before we were in a position to go into the box.

Cross-examination is always a trying experience. If conducted by a skilled Counsel, even for only an hour or two, it is something of a strain, and it is essential to be physically and mentally fit. I knew very well that when I went into the box in this case I would have to endure many hours of questioning. For a year beforehand I went into fairly strict training in order to be in good trim for the task. I lost between a stone and a stone and a half in weight and kept to a careful regime of diet and physical exercise. In the result, I was able to undergo continuous questioning (sometimes needlessly repetitive) without discomfort and hardship. Cross-examination is testing even if one knows all the facts and is minded to tell the truth. What it must be like if the witness is trying to cover up or to deceive, I do not care to contemplate.

Mr Justice Barker completely acquitted Begg and Lo on the grounds that there was no evidence of conspiracy against them. As regards the other four accused, the judge found that the charge as laid was 'bad for duplicity' and, in consequence, none of the four had a case to answer. That part of the judge's ruling was capable of being appealed and this took place in the Appeal Court in Hong Kong in November 1987. The judgment given on 19 November 1987 ruled that Mr Justice Barker's decisions in respect of the four were wholly defective. This did not mean that the accused would be subject to a retrial; their acquittals prevailed, but the Appeal Court judgement affected the costs which the four could reclaim from the Crown.

The judge's behaviour and judgment resulted in much adverse press comment for many weeks in London and Hong Kong. A typical example is the following short extract from the Far Eastern Economic Review, published in Hong Kong on 1 October 1987:

The conduct of the case and judgement by Justice Barker has given rise to disquiet within the judiciary ... The brevity of the judgement is seen not only as appallingly inappropriate to the significance of the trial. Worse, many argue, is that any decision to pre-empt the opinions of the jury after such massive submissions on complex issues by the prosecution is acceptable only if it is accompanied by a detailed analysis of the evidence and the legal arguments. Either Barker did not regard it as necessary, or preferred not to tackle what would have been a major task.

Also, Barker has been criticised for his conduct of the case itself. First, for his tendency to flippancy, evidenced even on the judgement day to greeting his wife from the bench and referring to his desire to visit Shek O Golf Club as relevant to the timing of the hearing on costs. A sense of humour among judges is an asset, and Barket is regarded as an amiable person, always convivial around the club bar. But in many eyes, the *gravitas* that the occasion demanded was sometimes lacking.

On a different note, some lawyers and judicial colleagues blame him in part for the inordinate length of time the prosecution case took. In his judgement, he said he had sympathy for (but did not accept) the argument that such a lengthy case made a proper result very difficult. Defence very successfully applied delaying tactics at every turn, with witnesses being questioned not just remorselessly but repetitively. But in addition to the laborious giving of evidence and lengthy cross-examination, no less than 195 days were devoted to legal arguments without the presence of the jury. These were almost all on technical points brought by the defence. In most case, Barker ruled in the defence's favour.

At one point, a ruling so constrained the ability of Lord Benson – Britain's most honoured accountant – to give his evidence that he exclaimed: 'What am I to do, my Lord, if the ruling conflicts with the oath I took to tell the truth. Do you wish me to abuse my oath?' Although the judgement came as a shock to the public, those who had been familiar with Barker's comments in open court and elsewhere had been predicting such a result months ago.

Other press comments of a virulent character appeared later and continued for some weeks. A senior member of the Bar in Hong Kong published an article which described the judgement as bizarre. Questions were raised as to how the judge came to be appointed to try this case. There was growing pressure in London and in Hong Kong for action to be taken. Finally, on 15 March 1988, Mr Justice Barker resigned his office.

The case had political importance. Under the original treaty, Hong Kong has to be handed over to the sovereignty of China in 1997 and the population of Hong Kong, which is wholly Chinese except for a relatively small proportion of expatriates, is very concerned about law and justice under the new regime. The population in Hong Kong is anxious that there should be a proper administration of justice when China takes over. When the case was first set in train it was the most important case of commercial fraud that had ever been tried in the colony and it was regarded as an example of how British justice should be conducted. It is clear from the press comment that the confidence of the people in Hong Kong in British administration of the law was undermined by the Carrian case.

I give below some account of the Roskill Committee which made suggestions as to how improvements could be made in the conduct of our criminal procedures in serious fraud cases. The work of that Committee was contemporaneous with the Carrian trial so that while the Roskill Committee was in session I had first-hand experience of the procedures ruling in the conduct of a criminal trial. This was invaluable from my point of view when we came to define our criticisms and to make suggestions for the future.

The Roskill Committee

I have already described in Chapter 9 the anxieties which were growing, in and out of the City of London, about the increase in commercial fraud in the United Kingdom and whether changes were required in existing legal procedures to enable fraudsters to be brought to book. One particular question was whether it was desirable for complex fraud cases to be tried by juries selected at random because of the difficulty which jurors have in comprehending the complexities of such cases.

In May 1984 a committee was appointed to consider this topic under the chairmanship of Lord Roskill, a Lord of Appeal in Ordinary. I believe that this decision owed much to the persistence of the Bank of England which was perturbed by the rising tide of fraud. There were eight members on the committee, which is a sensible and manageable number, of which I was one.

We set about it in the usual way by asking for submissions from responsible people or organisations whom we thought could provide reliable evidence. We also took oral evidence from a large number of people. I do not think that the public at large, and a large section of the legal fraternity, have realised the situation which has evolved in recent years. Fraud is a growth industry in the United Kingdom and it has reached alarming proportions. The majority of criminal trials are concerned with a well-defined event or events which can be clearly understood and comprehended by any person of average intelligence. I have in mind rape, murder, assault, burglary, theft and others of a like nature. Large-scale commercial fraud is quite different in character.

Fraudsters are often highly intelligent individuals. They exercise great skill in conducting their operations and may use companies or bank accounts overseas through which funds are channelled. These skills are used to conceal the substance of dishonest transactions by shrouding them in a form which makes them appear convincing to the layman. There is often a network of companies in which it is impossible to discover the identities of the beneficial owners. There may be an elaborate structure of agencies, contracts and accounts which make it difficult to discover whether it is a legal and honest framework designed to cope with complex trading and physical circumstances or a labyrinth designed to conceal deceit. Fraudsters know when to conceal the effect of the transactions by destroying, or deliberately refraining from keeping essential records so that the chain of events is broken and becomes difficult to follow through. They know every trick of the trade in the particular field of activity in which they engage and every loophole in the law. They do not hesitate to manufacture documents which justify transactions but in fact are often false or at any rate a shaded version of the truth. Usually they operate with one or two skilled accomplices, some situated abroad, which makes it difficult to decide when and where the critical decisions were made, or by whom.

When the case eventually comes to trial the juror is faced with many difficulties. He is initially likely to be unfamiliar with the procedure. There may be many defendants and multiple charges against each so he may have difficulty in remembering who is who and who is accused of what. The background against which the frauds are alleged to have been committed – the sophisticated world of high finance and international trading – is probably a mystery to most, or all, of the jurors, its customs and practices a closed book. Even the language in which the allegedly fraudulent transactions have been conducted will be unfamiliar. A knowledge of accountancy or bookkeeping may be essential to an understanding of the case, but if any juror has such knowledge, it is by chance. These factors demand special skills and the personnel concerned comprising investigators, judges, barristers, solicitors, accountants and jurors do not at present exist on anything like the scale which is needed. Changes are also needed in the conduct of the cases in court. None of this has yet been generally recognised and, until it is, fraudsters will continue to operate and escape conviction.

A primary consideration before the Committee was whether a jury selected at random can comprehend the issues in a complex fraud case which may last many days, and sometimes weeks or even months. With one dissentient the committee came to the conclusion that a jury in its present form could not be relied upon to do so. There were many reasons given for this decision in the report, but it is perhaps sufficient to give one only, namely that at present jurors are not required to be able to read or write English and they can be empanelled without the ability to do so.

The evidence given to the committee on this issue was divided down the middle. Some were in favour of abolishing juries altogether in complex fraud cases. Others, in equal strength, were in favour of retaining them on the ground that they were a 'lamp of liberty' or a 'bulwark of democracy'. It is surprising how often cases which are weak in logic are buttressed by highly coloured words which sound imposing but are in fact empty phrases. An interesting factor, however, was that many of those who favoured the retention of juries saw the obvious weaknesses and went on to suggest improvements such as a reduction in the number of jurors; a special jury chosen on the basis of education or background; a trial of three or five judges; or other variations. As it turned out the committee's majority finding was that in complex fraud cases the tribunal should be a judge together with two lay persons who were knowledgeable and experienced in business and commercial transactions; in other words we proposed a tribunal which was skilled and knowledgeable in the matters which came before it for trial.

When jurors were first called they were chosen from the people who could arrive at a decision by virtue of their knowledge of the accused. It was not until the eighteenth century that it was suggested that jurors should be independent people who would not have prior knowledge of the accused or the facts. Over the years it has become ingrained in the mind of the British public that juries are an essential feature of justice in all criminal cases. The prospect of bringing forward a measure in Parliament to change the jury system in complex fraud cases would probably fail. In the end it was no surprise that the government did not accept the Committee's recommendation. In the years to come, when the public begins to realise the special characteristics of complex fraud cases, and how unfitted many jurors are to undertake the task, it may be possible to introduce the necessary legislation. An added reason for so doing is that, in recent years, attempts have been made by accomplices of the accused to pervert the course of justice by subjecting jurors to threats and bribery.

The substance of the committee's report is given in the first paragraph:

The public no longer believes that the legal system in England and Wales is capable of bringing the perpetrators of serious frauds expeditiously and effectively to book. The overwhelming weight of the evidence laid before us suggests that the public is right. In relation to such crimes, and to the skilful and determined criminals who commit them, the present legal system is archaic, cumbersome and unreliable. At every stage during investigation, preparation, committal, pre-trial review and trial, the present arrangements offer an open invitation to blatant delay and abuse. While petty frauds clumsily committed are likely to be detected and punished it is all too likely that the largest and most cleverly executed crimes escape unpunished. The government has encouraged, and continues to encourage, ordinary families to invest their savings in equity markets, particularly in the equities of formerly state-owned enterprises. If the government cherishes the vision of an 'equity owning democracy' then it also faces an inescapable duty to ensure that financial markets are honestly managed and that transgressors in these markets are swiftly and effectively discovered, convicted and punished. Self-regulatory mechanisms designed to encourage honest practices are now coming into force. Where these mechanisms are used the law must deliver retribution, swift and sure.

Accordingly we made a large number of recommendations dealing with fraud from its inception until the trial closed. These involved the setting up of a special department (called the Serious Fraud Office) properly staffed with skilled accountants and lawyers to deal with complex fraud cases. We recommended proper training for judges and lawyers. We proposed a revision of the rules of evidence and the manner in which the case is presented in court. We urged properly conducted pre-trial reviews (which we called preparatory hearings) to define and limit the issues. We suggested the abolition of committal proceedings which we felt were time-wasting and unnecessary. We proposed the abolition of 'peremptory challenge' which gave each accused the right to exclude up to three people from appointment to the jury without assigning any reason.

The Roskill Committee stressed the importance of presenting cases clearly to the Court and the jury by the use of summaries, flow charts, diagrams and, when appropriate, visual aids. The importance of this is not yet understood, nor is it realised that it involves a skill and technique of its own, which requires much practice and the stimulating process of trial and error. Solicitors and counsel, on both sides of a fraud case, need to spend a great deal of time in the preparatory stages, long before the case comes to trial, in designing the shortest and clearest document or documents which will summarise the points at issue. Most frauds are, in essence, simple in character, but they are made complex by fraudsters who deliberately surround them with confusing detail or complicated book entries. The substance of the alleged fraud should, at the outset, be put down on paper in a few simple phrases, with the relevant figures, so that everyone in Court, at the outset, has a document in front of him pinpointing the precise nature of the fraud.

Much needs to be done in the use of visual aids, and nobody at the time of writing has been appointed to coordinate this new development by defining exactly what is required. In consequence, the differnt manufacturers of visual aids have not been given any authoritative guidance as to how or which pieces of their equipment can best be perfected. There are many differing interests involved – the Lord Chancellor's department, the Home Office, the police, the Crown Prosecution Service, the Serious Fraud Office, the Court staff, the Bar, solicitors and the judges – and their combined views need to be sought in order to bring about the equipment which will serve their collective interests best.

The government adopted the great bulk of the proposals which have now been incorporated in the Criminal Justice Acts of 1987 and 1988. In consequence the conduct of criminal trials in fraud cases will undergo radical changes in the next few years. Fraud will never be stopped but the improved machinery should help to check it and act as a deterrent.

The Joint Disciplinary Scheme

In the late 1970s there were a number of financial scandals in the City of one sort or another which led to public criticism. In some cases the role of the auditor or accountant was in question. The councils of the professional accounting bodies are sensitive to public criticism and towards the end of that decade felt that a determined effort should be made to enquire into such cases and to ensure that disciplinary action is taken if members of the profession have failed to carry out their responsibilities properly.

Accordingly, in January 1980 the three major accounting bodies in the United Kingdom (the Institute of Chartered Accountants in England and Wales, the Institute of Chartered Accountants of Scotland and the Chartered Association of Certified Accountants) formed a joint disciplinary scheme to take disciplinary action in any matter which gave rise to public concern. I was appointed chairman of the executive committee which administered the scheme and I held office for the ensuing seven years. I had a particular interest in it because of my interest in setting and maintaining standards in the profession, a subject which I have mentioned earlier (Chapter 6).

The scheme was additional to the disciplinary powers over its individual members which already existed in each of the three participating bodies and it may be asked why this special disciplinary procedure was set up. The reason is that the responsibilities of the accountancy profession involve auditing and other work which affects not only the interests of individual clients, but also the interests of the investing public who are not clients but who have a direct interest in the work we perform by reason of the substantial sums they have invested in listed and unquoted companies. The profession came to the conclusion that when a matter arose giving rise to 'public concern' which reflected adversely on professional or business conduct, the efficiency or competence of a member of a member firm, special disciplinary procedures should be brought into play. The scheme reflects the desire of the participating bodies to fulfil one of the obligations every profession owes to the community it serves, namely the need to maintain proper standards of work and behaviour by its members.

The method of operation was for the executive committee to appoint a committee of enquiry into any case which was brought it its notice by any of the participatory bodies as requiring investigation. In practice the committees of enquiry comprised two accountants and a lay person. After enquiry, the committee made a report and, if the report was adverse, penalties and sanctions were imposed either by the committee (in the case of a member firm) or by the parent body to which the member belonged (in the case of individual members). It is noteworthy that penalties and sanctions can be imposed not only on individual accountants but on the firms of which they are members. One of the sanctions was the right to require a person or firm to contribute to the costs of the enquiry. There was a right of appeal and in that event the executive committee appointed a separate appeal committee, the chairman of which was required to be an eminent lawyer. The reports of the committees of enquiry and appeal were to be made public in all cases so that any person could acquaint himself not only about the complaint, but the decisions made. As the years went by it was obvious that improvements in the operation of the scheme could be made and the executive committee made recommendations for that purpose to the participating bodies. The appropriate changes took place in 1987 but the basic purposes of the scheme have remained unchanged. Doubtless further improvements will be made.

This scheme is of vital importance to the profession because it makes clear to the members and to the public that bad work will not be tolerated. In some countries an undesirable practice has grown up of what is euphemistically called 'creative accounting'. For the most part this seems to me to circumvent the basic intention of established auditing and accounting standards. I believe that every country which has a professional accounting body of any size should set up a disciplinary scheme of this nature to curb these undesirable developments.

All those who accept office as members of a committee of enquiry or an appeal committee are paid at normal professional rates. In consequence the scheme was expected to be costly and so it proved in practice. The fact, however, that persons and firms in default are required to contribute to the costs is significant in keeping down the overall expenditure. It is necessary, of course, for the executive committee of the scheme to find responsible and experienced members of the profession and lay people to serve on the committees. In practice I never found any difficulty in doing so; this is a tribute to the three professional bodies and it indicates the importance of the scheme both to the profession and to the public.

The Open University

When I was on the point of retiring from Coopers & Lybrand in 1975, Lord Gardiner, a former Lord Chancellor, who was Chancellor of the Open University, asked me whether I would become Treasurer and I agreed to do so. I had, and still hold, a profound respect for the ideals of the Open University. It was an imaginative project. I think one of the special pleasures I got out of it was attending the graduation ceremonies when degrees were awarded. People from every walk of life ranging from those born to privilege and financial assurance, to those who had nothing to help them but their own determination and ability, had spent many hours in their own time to obtain a degree.

In other ways I was less happy in the environment. At that time the political affiliations of many of the staff were left of centre, sometimes aggressively so, and I found this unattractive in an enterprise which I believed should be politically neutral. For that reason I was not altogether sorry when my term of office expired. In addition the Treasurer's power to influence the financial expenditure was limited because the demands for resources were determined by the academic staff. Towards the end of my time I was embarrassed when it was discovered that some inaccurate financial returns, of which I was not aware, had been made to the appropriate government department. No loss of public money was involved but I was embarrassed by an event which should not have happened. The official concerned was a qualified accountant who was in due course disciplined appropriately by his professional accountancy body.

The Legal Profession in South Africa

At the end of 1987 I was invited to go to Cape Town in April 1988 to make what was described as the keynote speech at the first national conference ever held by the Bar in South Africa. I was not the first choice; this had fallen on one of the Law Lords but the government in the United Kingdom felt that a visit by a Law Lord in office to South Africa at that particular time would not be appropriate and might lead to unfortunate political incidents.

The subject on which I was invited to speak was the advantages or otherwise of the fusion of the two branches of the legal profession. It was one of the matters studied by the Royal Commission on Legal Services, and the Commission came to the unanimous conclusion in 1979 that fusion of the profession in Britain would not be in the public interest. For the year or two prior to the conference some sections of the solicitors' branch of the profession in South Africa had been pressing for fusion, and the government there had made enquiry into the possibility of supporting a change of this nature. These moves alerted the Bar to the need to probe the subject in depth.

During the conference the solicitors in South Africa appeared to change their ground. They said that they did not want fusion and believed that an independent Bar was desirable. At present solicitors may appear in the Magistrates' Courts, but do not have the right to appear in any of the Superior Courts and their claims were altered to asking for the right to appear in all courts.

I pointed out, when this revised claim was advanced at the conference, that, if solicitors accepted that a strong and independent Bar was necessary in the public interest, it was equally necessary to establish regulations and disciplines which would sustain the Bar in that form. If solicitors without the training, experience and the disciplines of the Bar were permitted to appear in the Superior Courts, they would not only do so, but they would be likely to prevail on their clients to let them do so. This would be particularly so in the simpler cases, which are the training ground for the younger members of the Bar in their earlier years; in consequence, the position of the Bar would be eroded. I do not know what the outcome of this controversy will be in South Africa, but an important principle is at stake if the future of the Bar is to be assured.

Virtually all the professions are continually seeking to raise their standards, to improve training and education (including post-qualification training); to tighten disciplines; and to increase specialist services in different branches of work. If the door is opened to allow people to engage in professional work who do not undergo the appropriate training, experience and educational process and are not subject to the related disciplines, the quality of the professions will obviously deteriorate. The Conservative government in the United Kingdom is continually pressing for restrictive practices to be removed and for free competition to prevail. This is a laudable project, but some restrictions are necessary in the public interest, and the only effect of removing them will be to debase the quality of service provided.

The situation becomes clear by analogy. An airline pilot is licensed to fly certain defined types of aircraft because he has been trained on those machines and has satisfied the authorities that he has had the necessary practical experience. It would be absurd for a pilot to say, 'I have a licence to fly a Piper Cub. I should therefore be allowed to handle any aircraft without further restriction.' This is, in effect, the attitude of the solicitors in pressing their claims for increased rights of audience.

During the conference I was asked to appear for a short time on the South African Broadcasting Service. In the course of the interview I was asked whether I thought the judiciary in South Africa delivered impartial and independent judgements. I said that it would be impertinent for me to express a view on this subject, but in the short time I had been in the country I had not heard anything to suggest that the judicial decisions were not impartial and independent. When the interview was over, the interviewer said, 'I hear what you say about the judicial decisions in this country, but that's not generally the view held here.' I was not then, and am not now, competent to express a view of this subject. The problem is that, in the panic of emergency legislation, some of the laws passed by the South African government are extreme. The judiciary are faced with the unenviable task of applying the law, because it is their duty to do so, even though some of them may feel that it is contrary to what citizens, black and white, are entitled to from the point of view of natural justice and established human rights. This is the situation which fosters disquiet in the mind of the public.

Before leaving for South Africa, I asked Professor Benney, the London silversmith, to make me a gavel, which I presented to the General Council of the Bar of South Africa to commemorate the first conference held. The gavel was an imposing article, with a silver handle, and I also put an inscription in silver round the base from chapter 40 of Magna Carta, which I have quoted in Chapter 10: 'To no one will we sell, to no one will we deny or delay right or justice.' It seemed to me that this sentence, which is remarkable both for its quality and for its economy of words, was appropriate for a gathering of lawyers, particularly in view of the situation I have just described.

The Minister of Justice in South Africa attended the session which I addressed and it was chaired by the Chief Justice. I concluded with these words:

'I end, as I began, on the precept enshrined in Magna Carta. Five hundred and fifty years later, with an equal economy of words, Pitt expressed the same thought: "Where law ends, tyranny begins." In any civilised country, therefore, it is the duty of government, and all of those engaged in the practice of the law, to ensure that every person has access to skilled advice, so that he may pursue or defend his legal rights without delay and, when appropriate, before a tribunal which is impartial.'

By these words, I was anxious to remind the audience that in these respects South Africa's recent record is not good. Under the emergency regulations existing at present (which do not seem likely to be withdrawn for some time) their citizens can be arrested without a warrant and held in custody without trial. Another disagreeable and disturbing fact emerged at a later point in the conference when it was stated that every year over 100,000 people, mostly black, are tried in the courts without any legal representation on their behalf. Conviction involved not only fines, but heavy custodial sentences. I do not care to think, by this process, how many people are wrongly convicted each year in South Africa, or have criminal sentences imposed upon them which are not fair.

The conference was well organised and my wife and I enjoyed meeting many old friends and making new ones. Attendance at the conference was for me also an emotional pleasure. I have described in earlier chapters how my father was originally a solicitor practising in Johannesburg, and I was pleased to be able to go back and (although I was not a lawyer) address the legal profession in the land of my birth.

After the conference was over we went to Durban where I

addressed the law faculty at both the universities in the city on 'professional standards'. We later moved up to Johannesburg, where I addressed a meeting of members of the Institute of Chartered Accountants in England and Wales who are resident in South Africa on the current developments in the accounting profession in Britain. I also spoke to the pupils of my old school, Parktown High School, on the merits of 'Thatcherdom' and said that I hoped eventually South Africa would breed a leader with the same indomitable qualities, who would lead them out of the political morass in which they are wallowing at present.

Directorships

The partners in the bigger firms of accountants do not as a rule accept appointments as directors of public companies, primarily for the reason that there may be a conflict of interest. A large firm has among its clients many public companies, some of whom are likely to be in competition. Those companies may well feel aggrieved if the person who audits their accounts and has access to all their affairs is in a position to influence the affairs of another company which is in competition. The second reason why such appointments are not accepted is that it is not sensible to spend time building up somebody else's business rather than one's own. In my own firm we adopted the policy of not accepting directorships unless there was an exceptional reason for doing so and a conflict of interest was unlikely to arise.

In 1953 I was invited to become a director of Finance Corporation for Industry Ltd. This was set up under the auspices of the Bank of England and the clearing banks to provide large-scale funds for industry which could not find the resources through the normal channels. It was an undertaking designed to help the resurgence of British industry and for that reason was considered to be an acceptable appointment. I remained on the board and its successor body, Finance for Industry Ltd (now Investors in

Industry plc or the 3i's as it is called), until I reached my seventieth birthday.

Also in 1953 I was appointed a director of the Hudson's Bay Company and in 1955 I was appointed Deputy Governor. This company began in 1670 under a Royal Charter. Its original purpose was to engage in trade with Canada and to exploit the natural resources of that country. It had a colourful and romantic history and, at that time, considerable glamour attached to its name. When I joined the board it was domiciled in London but in fact the great bulk of the business, apart from some fur sales made in London, was carried out in Canada. Over the long years of its existence the nature of its business has changed. In the early days many outposts were established in the north; they traded there and bought skins from the Eskimos and others in the area. These activities have continued to a greater or lesser degree, but the great bulk of the business in later years was represented by departmental retail stores in the major cities in Canada and in many of the smaller cities and towns.

I became less and less convinced as time went by that the board should sit in London when the great bulk of the business was conducted in Canada. I also felt that as directorships in London became vacant they should be filled (if the board remained in London) mainly by people who were experienced in the business of departmental stores and retail trading. Differences of view among the directors emerged and Lord Heyworth (who was appointed to the board after he retired from Unilever) and I resigned on those issues in 1962. A few years later the effective control of the board was changed appropriately. In 1979 the Hudson's Bay Company was taken over by the International Thomson Organisation in Canada.

In 1975, after I had retired from Coopers & Lybrand, I was appointed a member of the Hawker Siddeley Group plc which was led by an industrialist of exceptional ability, Sir Arnold Hall. In the course of this appointment I visited virtually all the subsidiaries in Australia, Canada and South

Africa and I learned much from my experiences. I retired when my term of office ended after my seventieth birthday because I felt that directors of public companies should not continue past the age of 70 unless the circumstances are altogether exceptional; there was nothing in my case to justify it.

These three directorships were invaluable to me in different ways. An accountant who spends all his time in professional practice does not always realise the pressures which are borne by the board of a company which is answerable to the public for the conduct of the company's affairs and is subject to constant comment in the press, often of a critical nature.

Epilogue

So ends this account of my life, which has been dominated by two factors. My mother told me that when I was born I was in such a hurry to get out into the world that the time spent in labour was very short and she was left completely exhausted. She said, without complaint, that some minor afflications she suffered in later life were due to my unseemly haste on this occasion. All my life I have been impatient to get on and finish any job that has come to hand.

The second motivating factor which has been with me since earliest memory is not the capture, but the thrill of the chase. This remains even now, when shadows are beginning to lengthen and faculties are diminishing. Nevertheless, I hope I shall always remain loyal to a prayer which I came across recently:

> Not the quarry, but the chase,
> Not the laurel, but the race,
> Not the hazard, but the play,
> Make me, Lord, enjoy alway.

Appendix: List of Some Special Assignments and Appointments

Sept. 1943 – July 1944 — Seconded from the Army to the Ministry of Supply to advise on the reorganisation of the accounts of the Royal Ordnance Factories and to carry out the reorganisation.

March 1945 — Released from the Army for government work and appointed Controller of Building Materials, Ministry of Works.

October – Dec. 1945 — Special three months' appointment to advise Minister of Health on housing production.

1946 — Returned to Cooper Brothers & Co.

1946 — Commander of the Order of the British Empire. (CBE).

1946 — Appointed independent member of the Linoleum Working Party – completed 1947.

1946 — Appointed member of the Advisory Committee to advise Ministry of Supply on the accounts of the Royal Ordnance Factories – completed 1950.

1947 — Appointed member of the Crawley Development Corporation (satellite town) by the Ministry of Town and Country Planning – retired 1950.

1947 — Appointed member of the Shipbuilding Costs Committee – completed 1949.

1947-48 — Memorandum and oral evidence submitted to Treasury Working Party 1947 and later memorandum and oral evidence submitted to Crick Committee 1948 (HM Treasury).

1948 — Member of New Towns Working Party on financial relations with local authorities – completed 1949.

1948 — Appointed member of the Committee to

enquire into the financial organisation of the Ministry of Food – completed 1950.

1952   Appointed member of the Royal Ordnance Factories Board – retired 1956.

1952   Appointed to a Committee to report on the cost of building power stations – Ministry of Fuel and Power – completed 1953.

1953   Acted as expert witness for the purpose of the valuation of shares held in the estate of R L Holt deceased.

1953   Appointed Deputy Chairman of Advisory Committee (the Fleck Committee) to consider the organisation of the National Coal Board and to make recommendations – completed 1955.

1953–62   Appointed Director of Hudson's Bay Company and Deputy Governor in 1955.

1953–79   Appointed Director of Finance Corporation for Industry Ltd.

1956   Appointed to the Council of the Institute of Chartered Accountants in England and Wales – retired 1975.

1956   Appointed member of Advisory Committee on Legal Aid – retired 1960.

1957   Appointed member of Tribunal under Prevention of Fraud (Investments) Act 1939 – reappointed 1966, retired 1974.

1957   Appointed adviser to Registrar of Restrictive Trading agreements in relation to cotton spinning and doubling.

1958   Appointed by Minister of Power to undertake on his behalf an enquiry into the methods adopted by the London Electricity Board for the disposal of scrap cable and into allegations made regarding those matters – completed 1958.

1958   Presented a paper to the autumn meeting of the Institute of Chartered Accountants in England

and Wales on 'The Future Role of the Accountant in Practice'.

1959   Appointed by Minister of Power to membership of a committee (the Wilson Committee on Coal) to review the work that has been done in recent years on the development of processes in which coal is the basic raw material and to make recommendations as to the direction of further research and development work and the type of organisation or organisations best suited to carry out such work – completed 1960.

1960   Appointed by Minister of Transport to membership of an advisory body to examine the structure, finance and working of the organisations controlled by the Commission and to advise the Minister of Transport and the British Transport Commission – completed 1960.

1961   Appointed by the National Coal Board to advise the Board on questions arising from the White Paper entitled 'The Financial and Economic Obligations of the Nationalised Industries' (Cmnd 1337 – April 1961).

1961   Appointed to investigate and report on the position of the railways in Northern Ireland.

1962   Presented a paper to the Eighth International Congress of Accountants held in New York on 'Auditing and the World Economy'.

1962   Appointed by the three Produce Boards (Meat, Dairy Products and Fruit) and the four shipping lines engaged in the New Zealand trade as chairman of a committee to examine the possibility of introducing economies in the shipping services; improvements in the procedures and shipping requirements of exporters and importers; and economies from palletisation and methods of loading and

	discharging cargoes – completed 1964.
1963	Appointed by the Chancellor of the Exchequer as a member of a committee to enquire into the practical effects of the introduction of a turnover tax (VAT).
1963	Appointed a Joint Commissioner to report on the proposed amalgamation of the British Employers' Confederation, the Federation of British Industries and the National Association of British Manufacturers leading to the formation of the Confederation of British Industry (CBI).
1964	Received a knighthood.
1964	Appointed a Joint Inspector by the President of the Board of Trade to make an investigation into the affairs of Rolls Razor Ltd.
1965	Appointed Vice-President of the Institute of Chartered Accountants in England and Wales.
1966	Appointed independent chairman of British Iron and Steel Federation Development Co-ordinating Committee to consider all aspects of iron and steel industry rationalisation and coordinated development.
1966	Appointed President of the Institute of Chartered Accountants in England and Wales.
1967	Appointed an independent member of the Permanent Joint Hops Committee by the Minister of Agriculture, Fisheries and Food.
1967	Appointed by the National Trust as chairman of an advisory committee to review the management, organisation and responsibilities of the National Trust.
1967	Appointed by the Joint Turf Authorities as chairman of the Racing Industry Committee of Enquiry to make a detailed study of the whole of the financial structure and requirements of the horse racing industry.
1967–81	Appointed a Trustee, 'Times' Trust.

1969	Appointed Vice-President of the Union Européenne des Experts Comptables Economiques et Financiers (UEC).
1969	Member of a committee to enquire into the administration and organisation of the Ministry of Defence.
1970	Independent member of the Royal Dockyards Policy Board.
1971	Knight Grand Cross of the Order of the British Empire (GBE).
1972	Member of CBI Company Affairs Committee.
1973	Appointed by the National Coal Board as a member of the team carrying out an independent enquiry into the purchasing procedures of the NCB.
1973–76	Chairman of the International Accounting Standards Committee.
1974–79	Appointed Director of Finance for Industry Ltd.
1974–79	Appointed Director of Industrial and Commercial Finance Corporation.
1974–75	Appointed by the Governor of the Bank of England to the City Liaison Committee.
1975–81	Appointed a director of the Hawker Siddeley Group plc.
1975–79	Appointed treasurer of the Open University.
1975–83	Appointed adviser to the Governor of the Bank of England.
1976–79	Appointed chairman of the Royal Commission on Legal Services to enquire into the provision of legal services in England, Wales and Northern Ireland and the organisation and structure of the legal profession.
1977	Received a Distinguished Service Award from the University of Hartford (USA) for work in relation to International Accounting Standards.
1979	Appointed chairman of the Executive

Committee of the Accountants' Joint Disciplinary Scheme to review cases involving public concern – retired 1986.

1981   Made a life peer in the New Year Honours. Introduced in the House of Lords on 11 February 1981.

1983   Elected an Honorary Master of the Bench of the Inner Temple.

1984–85   Appointed a member of the Fraud Trials Committee (the Roskill Committee).

1984   Honorary freeman of the Worshipful Company of Chartered Accountants in England and Wales.

1984   Centenary Award of the Founding Societies (Institute of Chartered Accountants in England and Wales).

1984   Elected to the Accounting Hall of Fame by Ohio State University, USA.

1985   Appointed Chairman of a Committee to consider and report to the President of the Institute of Chartered Accountants in England and Wales on the auditor's responsibility in relation to fraud.

1986   Made a Freeman of the City of London.

Index